Take a sentimental journey back through the hills and creek valleys of the Ozarks.

Hear tales of fiery preachers, moonshiners, and coon hunters—a way of life that is fading except in the memories of Jim Hefley and his boyhood home:

"We don't dig 'taters. We jist whack off the end of the row and lets 'um roll into the tow-sack."

"Our hollers air so steep, the hounds have to foller a fox one behind 'tuther, and wag thar tails up and down 'stead of sideways."

"If'un you could smooth Newton County out, hit'd be wider than Texas."

Way Back in the Hills

James C. Hefley

LIVING BOOKS
Tyndale House Publishers, Inc.
Wheaton, Illinois

Living Books is a registered trademark of Tyndale
House Publishers, Inc.

Living Books® edition

Library of Congress Catalog Card Number 84-52699
ISBN 0-8423-7821-9
Copyright 1985 by James C. Hefley
Printed in the United States of America
          10   11   12   13   14   15   93   92   91   90

For Mother and Daddy,
good and loving parents

CONTENTS

PREFACE
Who I Am and Where I'm From

Down in Newton County, Arkansas, we like visitors to come straight out and tell us their handle and business. So right off the bat, I'll identify myself as James Carl Hefley, the coon hunter's son. That's so you'll know I'm not James Carl Hefley, the postmaster's boy, my second cousin.

My daddy is Fred Joseph Hefley. I never heard where the Fred came from, but the Joseph is for his Uncle Joe Hefley, whom we called "Cross-eyed Joe" to separate him from the other Joe Hefleys, namely "Little Joe," "Big Joe," and "Shot Joe," also known as "Fiddlin' Joe." Shot Joe slipped on a rock, causing his old muzzle loader to discharge. The shot blazed through his temple, breaking a jawbone and forming a bulge behind an eye—thus he became Shot Joe. But when this Hefley picked up his fiddle and bow, folks forgot the frog's eye and thought of him only as "Fiddlin' Joe."

My grandfather, daddy's daddy, was Thomas Jefferson Hefley, a mighty hunter and prolific beekeeper. His father, my great-grandfather, was James Hefley, for whom I was named. He was known as "Grandpa Jim," "Uncle Jim," "Natty Jim," "Tradin' Jim," "Red Jim," and, in his old age, "Crazy Jim." Grandpa Jim's father, my great-great-grandfather, I was told, was Harv Hefley, who came to the Ozarks from Tennessee around 1850.

Hefley root diggers have run our ancestral name back more than 250 years to when the first ones sailed over from Germany. Today, you will find Hefleys in almost every big city telephone directory, but I'm concerned only with my immediate clan which populated Big Creek Valley in Newton County, Arkansas.

Newton County is in the heart of the Ozarks, where folks talk *Ainglish* that's closer to Shakespeare than some of the stuff you read in modern grammars. The old bard wrote: "Thou has spoken no word all this while, nor understood none either." Newton County people put it a little differently: "You'uns ain't never said nuthin' since ye come, nar understood none of whut we wuz sayin' neither." We had our own lingo, some from Old English, some tacked on along the way. We developed our own pronunciations, too. For example, wire is *w'ar,* fire *f'ar,* tires *tars,* and directly *dreckly.*

"Furriners" call Arkansas backwoodsy, when we've got Little Rock, Hot Springs, and Fort Smith. Citified Arkansawyers put down Newton County as the poorest, the rockiest, and the most backwoodsy county of the state. We admit to the rocky and mountainous parts. We only slightly exaggerate when we tell outsiders, with a sly grin, "We hold our cows by their tails so'uns they can feed along the ledges."

"We don't dig 'taters. We jist whack off the end of the row and lets 'em roll in the tow-sack."

"Our hollers air so steep, the hounds have to foller a fox one behind 'tuther, and wag thar tails up and down 'stead of sideways."

And, "If'un ye could smooth Newton County out, hit'd be wider than Texas."

Since you can easily get lost in Newton County, I'll have to guide you to Big Creek Valley. First, find the Buffalo River on a map as it wriggles west across the county like a king snake. Off the Buffalo, the creeks flow out of deep green valleys with rich bottom land, along which rise steep forest mountainsides, lined along the top by limestone bluffs. Big Creek flows into the Buffalo River from the south, fed by two forks of clear cold water about three miles above the mouth. We Hefleys lived along the east fork, although we never called it that. We always said "Big Creek" and referred to the west fork as the Other Creek. Folks on the western branch said the reverse. Confusing to outsiders, but it was all we needed to know.

You can find Ozark settlements named Needmore, Tightwad, Nogo, Jerk Tail, Hog Eye, Dry Knob, Hog Jaw, 'Possum Trot, and High Lonesome. No such scruffy names for us. Founder Ephraim Greenhaw named the main trading center on our Big Creek Mount Judea for the steep peak to the north and the Judea of the Bible. Mount Judea was too big a wad to chew, so we just called it Judy. One way of telling a "furriner" from a native is how he pronounces the name.

Judy squats on the side of a ridge two miles up from the fork of the creek. We Hefleys, along with other clans, were strung from Judy to the head of the creek, a distance of some eight miles. Uncle Elmer Hefley delivered our mail on a bay mare, six days a week for $480 a year, except when he wanted to go squirrel hunting. Then Aunt Viola—his "wom-ern," he called her—rode the mail horse.

The log house we all called "Grandpa's Place" stood about halfway along the mail route. My great-grandpa Jim's father-in-law built the original cabin before the Civil War, snaking great oak timbers from virgin forest with a mule team, hewing the logs square with a broad ax, notching them at the ends for a tight fit, and sealing the cracks with red clay.

Grandpa's place sat on the side of a pretty clover-filled meadow at the head of a short lane meandering up from the creek road. Younger Hefley families clustered around nearby hillsides within easy walking distance. We all gathered at Grandpa's place once or twice a week. While the men talked dogs and crops and the women gabbed over cooking and quilting, we cousins raced about the yard and meadow, playing Kick the Can and Stick Ball, and aggravating Grandpa Tom whose patience was thinner than a hound's ear. When we got hungry, we ran in for Grandma Eller's cookies and swigs of sweet milk. When it got so dark we couldn't see, we came in for supper, to be fol-lowed by singing and tale-spinning around the fire-place.

Here among my kinfolks and dozens of cousins in

Big Creek Valley I belonged. Here I felt secure in my identity as a member of the family that I believed to be the most important clan in the valley, county, state, nation, and world. Here is where I begin my true story of a boy growing up in the Ozarks.

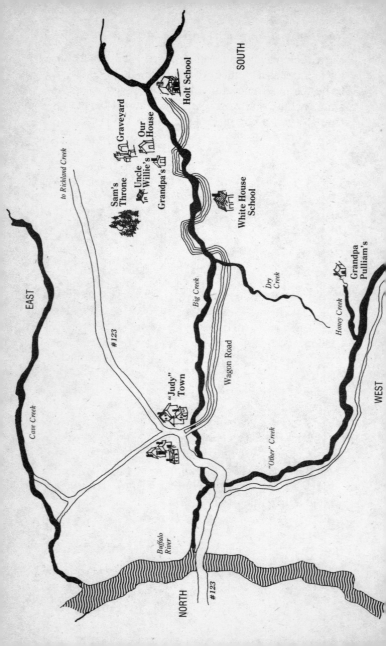

ONE
My Family Hero

Supper was over and a cold wind howled outside the old log house as a passel of grownups and kids gathered around the roaring fire in Grandpa's house. Grandpa Tom Hefley plopped into his favorite hickory-bottomed chair, tucked "Ole Betsy" under his chin, and picked up his bow. As he struck into "Sally Good'un," his old black cat jumped on one knee, purring and bouncing as his foot kept time with the fiddle music. The firelight and a kerosene lamp on the mantle cast flickering shadows across the log walls papered with thirty-year-old newspapers, as the sweet music filled the room.

Great-grandma Bett, Grandpa Tom's widowed mother, snug and warm in a long black dress that reached to her ankles, rocked on the other side of the fireplace from her fiddler son. I thought Grandma Bett must be the oldest person in the world. Lean and lanky, her angular face weathered by the hard years, she was our last living memory of the Civil War.

Grandma Bett had to be warmed up to talk. Some said that Grandpa Natty Jim Hefley had worn all the merriment out of her before he died. But by the time the dishwashers were in the front room and the babies snoozing on pallets, she was rearing to go.

"Tell us about the old 'uns, Grandma."

"Reckon there ain't much to tell, Chile. My daddy Thomas Jefferson Tennison, who built this cabin, and his two brothers come from Indianer. Down in Missouri he met a purty gal called Caroline. She was my ma. They had two young'uns before ever gettin' to Big Creek and four more atterwards. First, they lived on a little place below Judy, then Pa he comes up the creek and finds this good bottomland. Cleart the fields with his b'ar hands and built this hyar place. With a little hope from his brothers."

"Now Pa and Ma they warn't hyar very long till the tarrible war come on. Hit wuz a site to the devil, all the killin' and meanness that went on."

I perked up about this time. She was going to tell us about Grandpa Tennison, our Civil War hero. And Cap'n McCoy who led the Big Creek soldiers against the enemy.

"The Cap'n lived r'at down the creek, jist acrost from the Davis Farm. He wuz sarving in the Arkansas legislature when the fightin' broke out. He come home and raised a company of men, right hyar on Big Creek. Pa, he wuz thirty-six years old and had six chillern. He tolt my ma, "The Cap'n and the country needs me. I'm a goin' with my brother Dan'l to fight."

"Stoke up the f'ar, Tom. Hit's gettin' a mite chilly."

Grandpa Tom chucked a couple of logs in the fire-place, poked the coals to Grandma Bett's satisfaction, and settled back again with the rest of us.

"Now, whar wuz we? I'm gittin' so fergetful in my old age.

"W'al, we saw pore Pa ride off right down yander lane. Him settin' tall and straight in the saddle, and tarnin' at the creek road to wave good-bye. Ma, she says to us chillern, 'Take a good look at y'er pa. I don't know when we'll see him ag'in.' Pore Ma, she was tryin' mightily hard not to cry. Here she jist had her thirtieth birthday, with six chillern, and holdin' the youngest in her arms. And Pa ridin' off to war, with her not knowin' if he'd ever come back. That was an orful, orful sad time for all of us. Pa said he had to do his duty. Ma said while he was a doin' it, she'd keep the home f'ars burnin'. Folks did what they felt they ort to in them days.

"Pa, he rode off in March 1863, leavin' Ma and us older chillern to put in a crop and garden. 'Sides, Ma had all the cookin' and washin' to keep we'uns in clean clothes. And she had to look out fer them woods' outlaws who wuz too ornery and cowardly to go to war. They stole ever thang they could git their thievin' hands on whilst the real men w'ar off fightin'. Hit got so bad that some of the wimmern and chillern had to hide their foodstuffs in caves, and some most about starved.

"Cap'n McCoy hoped us as much as he could. Onct, he t'uk twenty wagun loads of people out of the county. We'uns didn't go, but we heerd that one of them waguns turnt a somersault over a river bank and landed bottom up'erds in a deep hole of water. The Cap'n had to bust the bottom open to git the people out.

"Only the good Lord got we'uns through that tarrible year. Pa didn't come back with the other boys. He was kilt at Pea Ridge, over fifty miles from his family, a fightin' fer his country."

She stopped and looked into the crackling fire as it if was too hard to go on. Then she said, "I mought as well tell ye chillern the truth. Ma tolt us later that Pa never got to enlist. They jist wouldn't let 'em in the Army, 'cuz he had T.B. and wuz a'coughin' and a'spittin' up blood. Tolt 'em to go home to his family. Hit was on the way back when Pa was kilt. That's whut Ma tolt us. We figured it didn't matter much whether Pa wuz on the roll 'er not. He died in the sarvice of his country. He wuz air hero."

We knew there was more to the story, for we had heard it before. "Tell us, Grandma, 'bout yer ma goin' to git yer daddy's body."

"W'al, when Ma, she heert Pa wuz dead, she said, 'I'm a goin' to Pea Ridge and fetch 'em home.' She hitched up the mules to the wagun and left us with kin folks. They thought she wuz crazy, but Ma, she'd made up her mind. Said, Pa wuz gonna be buried on Big Creek and that was hit.

"She found whair he had last been seed alive and asked around. A feller named Peel tolt her to go on back home and stop stirrin' up ole war wounds. This feller Peel could have kilt Pa, fer all Ma knowed. Ma said she warn't goin' without Pa's remains, if'un she had to stay all winter. She kept on until Peel took her to a grave and said, 'Thar's whar we put yer man.' Ma, she dug Pa up and brung him back hyar for burying. All that wuz left wuz bones."

I was only six or seven when Grandma Bett told about her family's suffering in the Civil War. She mentioned the names of others who had been killed, including Grandpa's brother, Daniel Tennison. But it was my own great-great-grandpa Thomas Jefferson Tennison, the namesake of Grandpa Thomas Jefferson Hefley, who stirred my blood. I imagined Grandpa Tennison pale and weak from coughing, riding into battle against the enemy, shooting enemy soldiers, until one brought him down. I saw my great-great-grandma Caroline Tennison going after his body in a covered wagon. I heard her arguing with the man Peel until he took her to Grandpa's grave. I sat by the fire at Grandpa's place and listened, believing my ancestor was the bravest man ever to set foot on Big Creek.

Grandma Elizabeth Tennison Hefley died when I was seven, but her stories lived on, passed down among the family, keeping pride strong among both the Hefleys and the Tennisons.

Years later, after World War II, the names of the Newton County men who had died in all the wars were chiseled on a monument beside the county courthouse in Jasper. Daniel Tennison's name was among them, but Thomas Jefferson Tennison's was not. I understood that this was because my ancestor had never actually been allowed to enlist in the Army.

My Michigan-born wife and I have often traded quips about old sectional allegiances. We thought it interesting that our respective states joined the Union the same year, 1836, as a political trade-off to admit one free state and one slave state. I bragged to people that our marriage was proof that a Rebel, whose ancestor had fought in the Civil War, and a Yankee with forebears on the Union side, could co-exist.

Well, we did argue occasionally. She thought the Confederate flag should be retired permanently. "We're all Americans. The Civil War is over. Done," she said. "We're at peace. Why keep bringing it up?"

"What's wrong with people showing their colors?" I asked defensively. "The Confederate flag stands for states' rights. That's still a live issue."

"It stands for slavery and a defeated army," she insisted.

"Watch what you're saying. My grandpa fought in that army."

If I had paid closer attention to politics while growing up, I might have attached some significance to Newton being a Republican county in a Democratic state. Or if I had dug a little deeper into Civil War history in college, I might not have been ignorant so long.

The truth came one cold winter day after Marti and I moved to a Chicago suburb. We were visiting new neighbors, the Taits. George was from Oklahoma, Helen from Madison County, Arkansas, which adjoins Newton County.

Helen showed me a new book. "A relative sent it to me," she said. "I thought you might be interested."

The engraving on the red cover jumped at my eyes: *History of Newton County* by Walter F. Lackey. I thumbed through looking for ancestors. There was

Great Grandpa Jim Hefley's name, also my daddy's, and many more familiar ones.

I borrowed the book and took it home. Later that evening I came to the section on the Civil War. I saw a picture of a man wearing a great white beard. Captain John McCoy, Big Creek's political leader, Grandma Bett had told us about him.

The Captain had served with distinction in the Arkansas legislature. And, and—what was this? Good grief! He had *opposed* secession and had gone home to Big Creek to organize a company of *Union* men! I recognized many of the names, including Daniel Tennison. Thomas Jefferson was missing, obviously, because he had been unable to enlist due to his tuberculosis.

Lackey said two-thirds of the able men in Newton County had served in the Union Army.

Marti saw my dazed expression and asked, "Did you find that one of your Rebel ancestors was a horse thief?"

"That isn't one bit funny."

"Did he do something worse?"

"Yeah," I muttered in chagrin. "He fought in your Union Army."

"You're kidding?"

"No. Looks as if most of the men on Big Creek did, too. I should have known. That's why Newton County has always been Republican. I never would have believed it."

"This is one to tell our grandchildren about." She laughed.

"Don't rub it in," I warned.

She smiled serenely and swept into the next room. She obviously found the information deliciously amusing.

Twenty more years passed, during which Marti never let me forget that my people had fought on the "right" side.

Not one to leave well enough alone, I set out to research my Ozark ancestors.

I searched the microfilm census files of the Arkansas State Historical Commission Library in Little Rock. There were all the Newton County Hefleys, except the pioneer, Harv Hefley. There were the Tennison families, including the widow Caroline Tennison and her six children. Elizabeth—"Grandma Bett"—was fourteen years old in 1870, when the first census was taken after the Civil War. She had been seven years old when her daddy went off to war, old enough to remember.

"Did you have ancestors who served in the Civil War?" a gray-haired librarian asked, seeking to be helpful.

"Well, not exactly," I explained. "My great-great-grandfather volunteered, but was not permitted to join because he had TB. On the way home he was killed by the Confederates."

"His sympathies were with the Union?"

"Yes, I discovered that much later. Newton County pretty much went with the North. My Michigan-born wife thinks it's very funny."

"We have the records on Arkansas soldiers who served in the Union Army," she said. "All we need to know is the name of the company. The men's records are filed alphabetically on microfilm."

From Lackey's history, I knew that Captain McCoy's was Company F, First Regiment of the Arkansas Infantry Volunteers, United States Army. I gave her that information and she put the proper roll on the projector I was using.

I spun the knob to reach the Ts and found my great-great-uncle, Daniel Tennison. The first entry announced his enlistment as a private: *March 10, 1863, Fayetteville, Arkansas, commanding officer, Captain John McCoy.*

The second gave his orders: *Detached as scout to Newton County, May 15, 1863.*

The third recorded his fate: *Cut off by the enemy and died of wounds while serving in Newton County, July 10, 1863.*

Perhaps there was another Tennison. I turned the knob again and there was my great-great-grandfather, Pvt. Thomas Jefferson Tennison!

He *had* enlisted on March 10 and had been sent on scout duty in Newton County, April 15, 1863, one month before Daniel.

The next item reported him "absent, supposed to be a prisoner." One more turn and I sat in shock:

August 22, 1863, Pvt. Thomas Jefferson Tennison failed to comply with orders of Colonel Johnson and was dropped as a deserter accordingly.

Grandpa, a deserter? My mouth dropped open in disbelief. Surely there had been a mistake. I turned to the final entry.

February 4, 1892. Application for removal of the charge of desertion and for amendment of record to show death in service has been denied.

Almost thirty years after his death, someone had tried and failed to get the record of desertion amended. Probably Grandma Caroline Tennison, who went for Grandpa's body, or one of the children.

I had become somewhat adjusted to the fact that my forefather had served in the Union Army. Now to learn that he was a deserter!

An echo came from the past: "We figgered it didn't much matter whether Pa wuz on the rolls, 'er not. He died in the sarvice of his country."

I checked the records of several more Big Creek Union soldiers and found other deserters. A familiar phrase caught my eye: "Failed to comply with orders of Colonel Johnson and was dropped as a deserter. . . ."

My ancestor was not alone in refusing to obey? What was that order?

Did it refer to the previous command: "Detached as scout to Newton County?" Where neighbor fought against neighbor and in some instances brother against brother.

Did he and the other "deserters" refuse to fight and kill their own neighbors and kinfolks who served with the Confederacy?

Was he killed at Pea Ridge, trying to get home to his starving wife and children?

Perhaps we'll never know the truth about the "hero" of our family.

That's the trouble with ancestors. You stand afar and peek back into the murky past. You want them heroic, noble, and famous.

What you find is what you get.

A thicket of unanswered questions.

Even when you keep believing.

As I do now in my Civil War grandpa, the hero of our family.

TWO
The Legacy of Grandpa Jim

The "character" of my family was Grandpa Jim Hefley, son-in-law of the Civil War soldier. His name—my name, James Hefley, is carved on the biggest tombstone in the Hefley family graveyard about a half mile up the mountainside from Grandpa's place.

My log house was much closer to the cemetery, which was just a few steps above the barn and next to our cornfield. Even in the daytime, when I was hoeing along the corn rows, I kept my back turned to the tombstones. At night I feared to look up that way from the yard.

I was scared of any graveyard, and especially this one, the final resting place of my great-grandfather. I think it was the countless stories I heard about Grandpa Jim who died the year after I was born, and the chilling "haint" yarns told by my uncles.

Uncle Willie Pink, one of Daddy's four brothers, could raise the hair off a dog's back as he told of seeing a ghostly figure in the graveyard, with eyes "lak a painther and a body ye could see plumb through."

We'd be sitting on the porch, on a hot summer night after supper, when Uncle Willie would start. By the time the mamas finished cleaning up, we younger cousins would be shaking as if we had chills. Then one of our mamas would come to the door, cock her ear, and scold, "You men air skeerin' these little chillern to death. They'll have bad dreams all night."

I often did. I'd be in the family graveyard by myself, with haints coming at me from every corner, and I couldn't get out. I still have occasional graveyard nightmares with Marti having to wake me up to keep from being kicked off the bed.

I don't blame all this on Grandpa Jim, but if half the stories I've heard about him are true, then you can understand. Ask everybody on Big Creek, old enough to remember, about Grandpa Jim. You'll get instant anecdotes and a mixture of opinions.

"Jim Hefley wuz the finest neighbor you ever lived by, but he took them spells," old-timer Elmer Campbell recalls.

"In a way he wuz off, and in a way he had lots of sense," someone else said. "Ye never met his match as a trader and talker. But he wuz high strung as a cat and flew around like a june bug."

"I was scared to death of him," a relative says. "We chillern would come around a fence row and there he'd be, settin' on a log in his long handle underwear, unbuttoned down the front. He'd be holdin' his stomach and lookin' like he was about to die.

When we appeared, he'd point his walking stick and say, 'I'm a'goin' to kill ye.' We'd take off runnin' like the devil was after us."

"Aw, Grandpa Jim, he didn't scare me when I was a boy," another remembers. "He made a lot of noise, but he wouldn't hurt a flea."

Grandpa Jim, I've been told, was the son of Harv and Adaline Criner Hefley. There's still a lot of mystery surrounding Harv Hefley. Uncle Bert Tennison, who died at ninety-eight, said Harv came to the Ozarks and changed his name because he had killed a man in Tennessee and was running from the law. Apparently he changed only his first name, because he had Hefley relatives in Big Creek Valley.

Grandpa Harv and Grandma Adaline Hefley may not have been legally married, since they are never listed together on the Arkansas census records. Only Adaline is recorded with children, James (Great-grandpa Jim), Solomon, William, Sarah, and Martha. There's an old story that Harv had two families, one in Tennessee and one in Arkansas, and two sons named Billy.

I'm in the line of James Hefley, the celebrated and controversial Grandpa Jim, my great-grandfather and namesake. He is the one everybody remembers, the one whom some believe cast a kind of curse upon his descendants.

What kind of man was he? I've asked the old-timers who knew him and four portraits emerge.

First there was "Natty" Jim—the spiffy, wiry, little red-headed dandy who cut a dashing figure at frolics and Baptist singings with the Widow Tennison's tall and lanky daughter Elizabeth (my great-grandma Bett).

They attended the Baptist Church, located near the head of the creek. Church records suggest it may have been founded around 1840 by young Reverend George Washington Baines, who was sent to the Ozarks by the Baptist Home Mission Society of New York City. Baines also served the Crooked Creek Baptist Church in adjoining Boone County. That church booted him out in a squabble. He moved on to Texas, where he is remembered as the great-grandfather of President Lyndon Baines Johnson.

While Jim and Elizabeth were raising their family, a preacher in the "New Restoration Movement" came into the valley and challenged the Baptists to put up a man for a debate. The result was a church split. The majority accepted the doctrines of the challenger and were baptized by him in the creek. They took the name Big Creek Baptist Church of Christ. "Baptist" was subsequently dropped and the descendants meet today as the Mount Judea Church of Christ.

The Hefleys and Tennisons went with the majority, with "Granny" Tennison (Elizabeth's mother), the last holdout in her family.

The second view of him was as "Tradin'" Jim, who bought and sold livestock and partnered with his cousin, Steve "Pelly" Criner to haul cedar logs to Buffalo River where they were floated downstream to a mill. By this and through judicious farming, Jim was able to buy Grandpa's place from his mother-in-law, and then extend his land holdings to become one of the biggest property owners in the upper valley.

He evidently gained the great respect of his neighbors, for they elected him Justice of the Peace of Big Creek Township in 1887.

Third, there was "Red" Jim, noted for his flaming red hair, that symbolized a hair-trigger temper that could be dangerous.

A drummer came up the creek selling hardware, medicines, and various knicknacks. Several women referred him to their husbands who were working for Grandpa Jim. The drummer came into the field without Jim's permission and began soliciting the men. Grandpa ordered him off his property. When the peddler came back, Grandpa got his gun. "I'm a'payin' these men fer their time. Jist back off and don't come back, 'er I'll drill yer carcass full of holes." After that the drummer restricted his sales to their homes.

Grandpa Jim became angry at the creek when a flood turned the channel across his cotton field. "I'm a'gonna put it back in its place," he announced. Neighbors told him it was impossible, but he started hauling rocks and snaking logs to a dam site at the point of diversion. "Uncle Jim, in spite of what ever'body tolt 'em, turnt the creek back into its ole channel," recalls neighbor Mitchell Hefley. "If'n he intended doin' sumthin', nobody could talk 'em out of it. He didn't take a back seat to nobody. An' he'd tell ye jist whut wuz on his mind."

After Harv Hefley's death, the place where Jim was raised went to the Criners. When they started tearing down the old house, Jim let them know he didn't like it.

Pelly didn't take him seriously and came by the barn where Jim was shoeing a horse. Jim told him to leave and turned back to his work. Pelly, a bit of a prankster, grabbed a horseshoe and nailed it to a stump. When he saw Jim turn around, he jumped on his horse and rode away laughing.

Grandpa ran for his gun, took aim and fired. As the horse fell dead, Pelly jumped to safety and ran for the sheriff.

But the sheriff could not find where the bullet went in. He arrested Jim anyway and put him on trial. Jim hired a lawyer who argued that there was no proof his client had killed the horse because they had been unable to find a bullet.

"'Course we couldn't find a hole," the prosecutor declared. "That bullet entered the horse's rear end." The jury collapsed in laughter and voted the defendant not guilty on the basis of lack of evidence.

Grandpa Jim had a reputation of minding his own business, and he expected neighbors to mind theirs. He ordered his sons to keep out of the feud between the Nicholses and the Smiths. "'Hain't no reason none of us should git kilt," he said.

One day Jim and his boys were at a dinner honoring the patriarch of the Nichols family, "Uncle Marion." The Smith men rode up and started making threats.

"We're a'goin' home," Jim announced. They were barely out of sight when shooting erupted. The Nichols men barricaded themselves in Marion's cabin.

After awhile Tom Nichols came out waving his hands in the air, calling for peace. Young "Toad" Hefley, the son of Jim's first cousin, foolishly walked beside him. A rifle cracked and Tom fell dead. "They've kilt Uncle Tom," Toad screamed.

The Smiths leaped on their horses and headed for home with the Nichols men in hot pursuit. A shotgun blast caught Jim Smith in the hip. A relative snatched him up and carried him to a cave near the forks of the creek. He died in the cave a few days later.

The next time Grandpa Jim saw Toad, he hollered, "You could have been kilt, boy. Next time, git out of the way of somebody else's fightin'."

The feud persisted for years, with several more being killed. But Grandpa Jim stayed out of it.

Jim Hefley prospered while Grandma Bett gave him four sons and four daughters. Thomas Jefferson, my daddy's father, named for the Civil War soldier, was followed by William, Sarah, Cynthia, Rosa, Mary Jane, Albert, and Joe.

Albert, while a teenager, developed an infection in his ear. A boil or tumor formed and ballooned his head into a monstrous shape. No doctor, no medicines could bring down the swelling.

Grandpa Jim selected the burial site on the hill. After Albert's funeral he built a small house over the grave. For many days afterwards, he refused to work, going to his son's grave to mourn.

Then a beloved eleven-year-old grandson, Dennis Holt, fell and severely injured his leg. When the leg started turning green, the family sent for doctors to amputate. The boy died a few days later and was buried beside young Albert. Grandpa Jim led the mourning.

Not long after the boys died, Grandpa Jim began complaining of stomach pains. "Hit's like my gut's a'f'ar," he moaned. Some days the pain became so great that he screamed in agony. People passing on the creek road came running and asked Grandma Bett if they could do anything. No one, not even the country doctors, could ease his torment. Some speculated that he had been bitten by a mad dog.

One minute he was "barnin' up" the next, "freezin' to death." When hot, he stripped down to his underwear and splashed in the creek. When cold, even on a July day, he made Grandma Bett build a roaring fire. He lay stretched on the hearth before the fireplace, a hot iron wrapped in a sack pressing against his stomach, groaning in anguish.

Day after day this went on. When Grandma Bett saw company coming, she tried to quiet him down. "Hesh up, Jim, they'll think ye'er crazy."

He took to wandering up and down the creek road and scaring children. But when grandchildren came to the house, he turned pleasant. He had saved a jar of dimes from which he paid them to cut wood and pick berries.

Grandma Bett treated him like a child. It seemed she could never make him content. For one thing, when her stockings would come down, he'd yell, "Pull up yer socks, womern."

One day he shouted, "F'ar in yer socks, Bett!" and pitched a shovelful of coals at her feet, with some of the fire landing in her stockings. She screamed and danced around the room, clawing at her shoes.

The children decided something had to be done. His sons took him to the state asylum in Little Rock. The doctors kept him there a few weeks and then sent word to his family to come and take him home.

One day he was caught pointing a gun at a neighbor. The boys took him back to the asylum. A few days later word came that he was no longer welcome.

"The way he complains and rattles his guts," the doctors said, "he's driving us crazy."

"Pore ole Jim," people said in the valley. "Pore ole Crazy Jim."

Yet one day Elmer Campbell was helping son Tom kill a hog. As they were getting ready to hang the carcass on the scale, Elmer asked, "How's yer pa doin'? Is he still actin' crazy?"

"I'll show you how crazy he is," Tom said, and called his father out of the house.

"Pa, look at this hawg and tell us how much ye think it weighs."

He guessed the weight to the pound. Then before Elmer left, Jim said, "I've heard of a calf for sale down the creek. If I give ye the money, will ye go and buy it for me?"

But the next day he was screaming in agony.

The bad spells got longer, the good days shorter. In his seventy-sixth year, after a long spell of crying in pain and unable to pass waste, he expired. The country doctor said he died from "locked bowels."

They held his funeral on the porch of the old house, then loaded his coffin into his wagon, and hauled him up the hillside to the graveyard he had picked for Albert. Later the family put down a tombstone, marked with his vital statistics and the words,

"GONE BUT NOT FORGOTTEN."

As a child I heard stories about him that have now been confirmed in more detail. But I didn't learn until last year about the strong belief among some in the family that he left a legacy of mental illness and depression to be passed on to his descendants, especially the males.

I was visiting with an older cousin last November. We were talking about recent deaths in the family, including one possible suicide. "You know it's that depression," she said. "You know it comes from Grandpa Jim."

I didn't know. She then cited about a dozen persons, some dead, some living, as proof.

On further investigation, I learned some of the depressions had been preceded or accompanied by heavy drinking. Still, I heard kinfolks declare that the depressions were inherited from Grandpa Jim. "You might be strong enuf to escape it, but you're shore liable to git depressed if you're in the family," one cousin said. Yet others declared such talk was "dangerous." "If it gets on your mind that you're going to be depressed, then you're going to be depressed," another declared.

Dr. Billy Frank Hefley is my second cousin, descended from Grandpa Jim through Uncle Bill. Through his mother, he is also in the Criner line. Billy Frank has practiced medicine in Little Rock for many years and is one of Arkansas' most respected physicians. On my next trip back to the Ozarks, I stopped and spent the night with him. I asked him his opinion of Grandpa Jim's ailment.

"Grandpa could have just been a poor old sick man with cancer. The cancer could have caused the intestinal obstruction that they called locked bowels. For that matter, any number of diseases could have affected his abdomen and given him pain. Obviously something hurt him, and nobody back then knew what it was."

What about the trips to the asylum?

"Here's an old man on Big Creek, sick, crying with pain, with very little medical care available. His family is perplexed. They thought of Little Rock as the center of the state, so they naturally brought him here. That doesn't mean he was mentally ill."

Could severe physical pain have driven him into depression?

"Yes, you can become depressed in response to a real life situation.

"Or, the cancer could have metastasized his brain and affected his mind."

I talked to Dr. Ross Campbell, a psychiatrist friend in Chattanooga. "How many descendants does your Grandpa Jim have?" he asked.

"Oh, two, probably three hundred, maybe more. I haven't counted them."

"How many depressions are you aware of?"

"Twenty, maybe twenty-five that we know of."

"That's less than average for a random sample of the population. I can't see what all the worry is about."

I've made the rounds of scores of kinfolks, finding both believers and disbelievers that our family is predisposed to depression.

One cousin admitted to having suffered a severe depression. "I used to believe that my depression was inherited from Grandpa Jim," he said. "I had also been drinking heavily. I found that when I quit drinking, my depression soon lifted."

I shared with him an experience of once being depressed after an accident. "How did you get out of it?" he asked.

"I went to see my family doctor. He found my blood pressure a little high. He advised me to get off my duff and start an exercise program. I took up running.

"I also exercised a little faith in the Lord," I added. "I believed God was going to help me get better. I did."

"Weren't you worried about the 'curse' from Grandpa Jim?" He smiled.

"I didn't know about it then."

"Good thing you didn't." He grinned.

THREE
Daddy Was a Coon Hunter

When Grandpa Jim Hefley died, Mama and Daddy and I were living in a little shanty three miles up the creek from Grandpa's place. Grandpa Tom and Grandma Eller Hefley moved from the log house on the hill near the graveyard to the old place in the creek meadow. We moved into the house where Tom and Eller had raised their eleven children.

Everybody said Grandpa Tom looked like Grandpa Jim, except his hair and moustache were not quite so red. Like his daddy, he had a short fuse, especially with grandchildren when they were running about, getting into trouble.

If you were around the house when he was outside, you could hardly breathe without him hollering. "Shet that gate!" he'd yell. "Stay out of the smokehouse!" "Git out of y'er grandma's garden!" "Leave my ole dawg alone!" "Stop pullin' my cat's tail!" "Git away from my bee gums!" "Don't go in the cellar!"

"Git out of my apple tree!" "Don't throw y'er ball in the yard. Ye'll break a winder!"

When I didn't pay attention, he'd sting my behind. I'd go runnin' to Grandma Eller and she'd pick me up and kiss my cheeks.

"Now, Chile, Grandpa don't mean you no harm. Jist try and stay out of his way."

On a Saturday night we'd gather around the fireplace and Grandpa would get out his fiddle and grin. He'd push the old cat off and take me on his lap and squeeze. Then he'd put me down and strike up a tune. I soon forgot any hurt feelings.

Grandpa Tom never did act crazy like his daddy. Neighbors spoke well of him. He was known for keeping his word and providing for his family. He taught Sunday school in the Church of Christ and read his Bible a lot. If he'd just had a little more patience with grandchildren! Maybe it was difficult because there were so many of us and so many ways we could cause him trouble. I mean, with a big orchard, eight or ten hound dogs, sixty or seventy bee gums, plus cattle, hogs, chickens, and ducks— well, what could you expect with twenty to thirty kids chasing around the meadow, yard, and barn lot?

Bless the memory of dear Grandma Eller! If she wasn't cooking for company or the dogs, she was sweeping, picking up, wiping noses, and reassuring us that Grandpa hadn't meant what he said. All while she had a terrible heart condition, swollen legs, and, according to Doc Sexton, was living on borrowed time.

And yet every night if you stayed awake long enough, you could hear her thanking the Lord for his blessings and her family, sometimes naming a dozen people, and asking God to let her live until "my chillern 'er all raised." When I came along, she had about reached that goal. She had only Aunt Bess and Aunt Alta at home, and both of them were sparking.

Grandma Eller had a hard coming up herself. Her mama died in Texas, leaving Grandpa Guthrie, her blacksmith daddy, with three children. Eller was just eight; Fanny, only eleven; and their brother, Pink, was twelve. Uncle Willie Pink, my storyteller uncle, is named for him.

Their daddy couldn't make a living in Texas, so he hitched up his oxen to a wagon, put his kids and tools in it, and turned back east. I've never heard who directed him to Newton County, except that he followed an old road into Cave Creek Valley and set up his blacksmith shack beside the wagon. No relatives. No money. Just his tools, a few pots and pans, and three hungry little kids sleeping in a wagon.

Not long after they arrived, neighbors heard the little kids crying and found him dead on the ground beside the wagon. He may have died of a broken heart over the loss of his wife and his not being able to take care of the children.

"Aunt" Delly Davis, who lived a couple of miles down Big Creek from Grandpa's place, heard about the homeless children. "A body can't let three little chillern die in the wilderness," she said. She brought them to Big Creek and got Aunt Sarah Greenhaw to take the girls. Then—I never learned how the connection was made—a wealthy lawyer in Little Rock came and got Pink and supported him all the way through college.

Pink Guthrie grew up in Little Rock, moved to Texas, had a successful career in insurance, and raised a fine family. Fanny married "Stagger" Bill Hefley and had seventeen children in Big Creek Valley before moving close to her brother in Texas.

Grandpa Tom took a liking to little Eller. When he was seventeen and she fourteen, he got into a fight at school. He walked right in, pulled Eller up and said, "Hit's time we wuz gettin' hitched."

They rode down the creek looking for the JP, who had succeeded Grandpa Jim. Just before school was to dismiss, the teacher saw them coming back on the horse and told his pupils, "Everybody go to the door and wave to the newlyweds."

Grandma had triplets the first time. All died. Six girls and five boys followed. My daddy was the fourth youngest.

Daddy took his gentle ways after Grandma Eller. I never heard him raise his voice to me or any of my brothers and sisters. When he lost patience, he just fell silent or walked away.

He took his love for hunting and fishing from Grandpa Tom. Hardly a day passed without Grandpa Tom taking to the woods for a squirrel. Three or four nights a week he went out for 'possum and coons with a son or son-in-law. Daddy, I've heard, ran behind Grandpa from the time he was a little boy.

Mama's name was Hester Hosanna Foster before marriage. She was brought up in a cabin in the woods. She was a schoolteacher before she married Daddy. She didn't care all that much for her man being in the woods and on the creek bank four and five nights a week.

Our log house—the one which Daddy got from Grandpa Tom—was smaller than the one at Grandpa's place. It was off the road and above the creek about half a mile. Smaller than the old house in the meadow built by Grandpa Tennison, it had just one big room and fireplace with stairs climbing to a sleeping loft and a lean-to kitchen in back where Mama cooked on a small cast-iron stove.

When the days began getting longer in the spring and the garden work was done, Daddy dug a can of worms at the barn lot. Tin cans were precious, but he kept one just for fish bait. He had Mama fix an early supper, then we walked down to the creek road. Mama went on over to Grandpa's place and visited while Daddy and I scrambled down the little bluff and sat on the round rock that overlooked our favorite hole.

We sat there, side by side, holding our sycamore poles, fighting off the gnats, waiting and watching and listening. Velvety darkness stole over the blue water. Bullfrogs harrumphed from beneath willows on the far bank. Crickets and katydids chirruped in leaves left over from winter. Whippoorwills warbled and owls hooted in the tall trees. What a grand band to entertain father and son while the fish were making up their minds!

One evening we were there when, thump! My pole dipped. "Daddeeeeee! Daddeeeeee!" He grabbed my sycamore and pulled out a goggle-eyed perch the size of his hand.

He strung the fish and things got quiet again. Directly, his pole dipped and he pulled back. "Got me a big 'un, Son! Git back, git back! I don't know what it is!"

He hauled the creature out kicking and splashing and dragged it up the bluff to the wagon road that ran along the top. In the lantern light I saw what he had. "Eel! Eel!" I squealed as the snakelike, slimy denizen thrashed under Daddy's hands. After "Daddeee" and "Mommeee," "eel" was the first word I had ever spoken.

When I was a little older he started taking me squirrel hunting in the early morning or late afternoon. Then he let me accompany him for 'possum and coons at night.

He'd say, "Do you wanna go, Son?" I nodded my little black head. "Do ye think ye kin keep up?" I kept nodding. "OK, git yer coat."

By this time, I had a little brother. "Me go, me go, me go," Howard Jean would beg, toddling after us, and Mama would pull him back. "Fred, don't you keep James Carl out too late," she begged.

He'd answer, "Oh, we'll jist go up the holler a ways." Some nights we were two in the morning getting home.

One night, when I was about seven, Ole Lion, the spotted hound, and Ole Muse, the coal black cur, hit a hot coon trail in the hollow. Daddy took off running, lantern swinging, yelling, "Come on, Son." As usual, he never looked back. I came crashing through the brush after him, trying to keep close to the light.

"Yooooo! Yoooooo!" Ole Lion had treed. "Yoooo! Yooo!" Ole Muse joined in.

I ran up panting behind Daddy, who had stopped at the foot of a tall white oak. Setting his lantern and gun down, he threw the spot from his five-cell flashlight from limb to limb, looking for eyes. Finally he spotted a hole in the tree trunk about thirty feet up. "He's in thar. Shine the light so I kin see to climb up."

I took the light and he jumped for a low limb, pulled himself up, grabbed another limb, and kept going until he got near the den. Then he broke off a tree branch and rammed it in the hole.

Pfitttt! Pfitttt! That old coon jumped out, almost knocking Daddy out of the tree. It ran out on a limb, leaped to a lower one, then pitched to the ground, landing on Ole Lion's back and grabbing the hound's ear. "Yipe! Yipe! Yipe!" Ole Lion screamed, dancing around, trying to shake Mr. Ringtail off. Ole Muse came roaring in for the rescue, grabbed a piece of fur, and the coon and two dogs went rolling down the hill. Daddy scrambled down from the tree and ran after them with lantern and gun, with me carrying the flashlight and tumbling at his heels.

Mr. Ringtail got free and scrambled up a hickory. Daddy grabbed the flashlight from my hand, spotted him on a limb, gave the light back to me to hold, took aim, and fired his rifle. The coon plummeted straight to the ground. "Git away, dawgs! Git back!" Daddy grabbed the dead animal, plopped it in a tow sack brought along for the purpose, and we went on for another one.

We didn't get a coon, or even a 'possum every night. Sometimes the dogs would hit a trail and run out of our hearing. "We'll build a f'ar an wait," he'd say. The dogs might be three hours coming back, but we stayed put. One night there was a light snow on the ground. We waited and waited. I dozed off under a covering of leaves. When I woke up, Daddy was covered with white and snoozing by a log.

Mama was awake when we got home. I crawled in with Brother under a heap of covers, my feet like blocks of ice. "Don't wake the baby," Mama warned. "I had hard enough time getting him to sleep."

When fur season came in November, Daddy set a trapline. Every couple of days he would "run" the line to collect what had been caught and to rebait the traps. I went with him except when we had company.

One Saturday Uncle Vester and Aunt Leathea and their children were visiting. Daddy and Uncle Vester went to run the trapline, leaving Utah, their oldest son, to play with me. We had a great time bouncing in the hay loft and knocking wasp nests off the rafters.

About sundown, Mama called us in for supper. We were just sitting down to cornbread, milk, beans, and greasy possum when we heard dogs barking and Daddy and Uncle Vester talking excitedly. Utah and I ran to the door and heard an unearthly "Waaaa-oooweeee! Waaaoooweee!" The screeching was enough to curdle your blood. Like a dozen old tomcats screaming in unison.

"You young'uns stay back in the house!" Mama shouted. "Get your little brother, James Carl. Don't let him out the door."

I pushed Brother behind me and ran across the porch and into the yard with Utah. Daddy and Uncle Vester were easing a long pole to the ground. They had a wildcat stretched out and tied around the pole. It was about as big as Ole Lion. The dogs were baying and circling and Daddy was kicking them back.

Mama saw it from the door and was speechless. Daddy had brought home a live coon and a live fox before, but never a wildcat, an animal powerful enough to rip open a person's stomach. "What in the world?" she gasped. "Fred, Vester, have you men gone crazy?"

"Aw, he's jist an ole wildcat, Hester. Caught 'em in a trap. Maybe we kin make a pet out of 'em."

Daddy's little-boy grin didn't amuse Mama in the least. "Fred, shoot that animal right now, 'fore it hurts somebody."

"Aw, we're gonna keep 'em alive a day or two. See how he fares."

"Well, where do you intend to keep it? In the house with the kids?"

Daddy already had a chain around the big cat's neck and was fastening the chain to a post in the yard fence. "We'll tie 'em hyar fer now. The dawgs know not to git too close."

Daddy snapped the chain and jumped back. The wildcat leaped, snarling and clawing the air, jerking the chain against the post and falling back in a heap.

"Git away boys! Stay out of his reach!" Daddy pushed Utah and me back on the porch.

Poor Mama just about went crazy herself. She fussed and raved and did everything but cry. Finally she saw Daddy was not going to be moved and got everybody to the supper table. Daddy only said, "We'll put it in the barn in the mornin'."

The next morning Daddy and Uncle Vester tied the wildcat on the pole and took it to the corn crib. That night while we were down at Grandpa's place the animal ripped the chain away and escaped. About a month later I was at the spring getting a bucket of water when I happened to glance across at a cedar nearby and saw a skeleton. The poor wildcat had caught its chain on a root and, in trying to get away, had run round and round the trunk of the small tree until it probably choked to death. When Daddy and I told Mama what had happened, she sighed. "At least it didn't hurt none of us. Fred, please don't ever bring such an animal home alive again."

Mama didn't raise much fuss about trapping and hunting during fur season because the hides earned cash money. Except she didn't like Daddy dropping the dead animals in the house when he came home from hunting. He picked them up before breakfast and called me into the backyard while he removed the hide. He turned the hide inside out and stretched it over a board with the hair next to the wood. The boards were hung in the smokehouse beside the hams to dry until he had enough to take to Judy and sell. A 'possum brought about fifty cents, a skunk a dollar, a coon or fox about two dollars, and a mink was a prize that fetched upwards of twenty dollars. He earned one to two hundred dollars each winter.

From this I got new denim overalls, coat, shirt, a pair of high-topped shoes (I went barefooted from March till November), a suit of long handle underwear, and a "boggin" (toboggan) cap. Daddy and Howard Jean got about the same, with Mama getting a new dress, and money left over to buy lard, sugar, salt, and flour to last throughout the year. We didn't have much money in the mid-thirties, but it went further than it does today.

Life wasn't all hunting and fishing. Morning and evening I helped feed the chickens and animals. Then Daddy milked while Mama fixed the meal.

One evening Daddy was filling the bucket while the old cat sat on its haunches to the side, hoping for a squirt. I failed to fasten the latch on the horse stable. Ole Babe, our mare, came out before Daddy realized what was happening. The horse kicked the cow, the cow kicked over Daddy's milk bucket, and the cat got drenched.

I was too young then to know about horse breeding. Later I learned that Daddy paid Oscar Daniels thirty dollars for his stud's services to Ole Babe. I noticed when her flanks began swelling and asked Daddy if she was sick or something. "No, she's got a colt growing in her," he said.

On the wild and stormy night of April 24, 1934, Daddy went to the barn after supper and didn't come back until after I was asleep. Next morning he pulled me out of bed. "Come up to the barn and see the new colt."

The little critter was standing up, nuzzling its tired-looking mama. "That was in her belly?" I asked incredulously.

"Yep, that's what made her look so big."

"How-how did it git in thar?"

"Hit jist grew."

"W'al what started it growin'?"

"I'll 'splain that to ye some other time, Son. I think yer mama needs ya back at the house."

"Fer what?"

"She jist needs ye. Now go on."

Ole Timbrook outgrew his mother. With his gleaming red coat and matching blaze that complemented the trim around his ankles, he was a beauty. After he was grown, I noticed that men kept bringing mares to his pasture. I wanted to go see, but Mama always had something for me to do in the house. Finally Daddy said, "Hester, he's got to learn sometimes. I'll see that he don't git hurt." That wasn't what Mama was worrying about. I won't describe it, but Ole Timbrook's "performance" was impressive to a seven-year-old boy.

Ole Timbrook earned us twenty dollars for every successful stud service. Daddy kept his coat shiny and trim and seldom hitched the stallion to the plow. I was under strict orders never to try to ride him. One day, when I was leading him to water, the temptation became too great. I shinnied onto his bare back and yelled "Giddap!" About a hundred yards from the spring he smelled the water and took off, with me bouncing on his bare back like a soap bubble in a whirlwind, pulling back on the rope bridle and screaming, "Whoa, Timbrook, whoa!" He jumped a log, heaving me over the side. I fell under his hoofs, barely escaping being trampled, but lacerating my scalp on a rock. With blood pouring down my neck, I ran home shrieking. Mama saw me and almost died of fright before she got the bleeding stopped.

Around April Daddy hitched up Ole Babe to the turning plow and broke up the corn patch that lay along the backside of the graveyard. After he carved out furrows, he and I walked side by side, planting the seed corn. I walked on the side away from the graveyard. No sense tempting the ghost of Grandpa Jim.

Then when the green shoots got a few inches high, he plowed between the rows and I came behind, hoeing out the weeds between the corn.

"You spend half the time lookin' at the sun," he said as he passed me.

"I jist want to know how long it is until dinner time," I replied.

"When the sun gits straight up, we'll eat."

"I know, but it moves awful slow."

"Well, don't look up, and the time'll pass faster."

I never did like hoeing corn.

The corn had to be hoed and plowed twice before it was "laid by" until fall. Then we took out the harvest. The ground was too steep and rough to bring a wagon into our cornfield. We couldn't have afforded one anyway. What we had was a kind of poor man's wagon, actually a big sled, with boards connecting the runners and wide planks nailed along the sides to keep the corn from falling out. Ole Babe pulled the sled along as we jerked the corn off the stalks and pitched it in.

We filled the corn crib and saved the best ears for grinding. After supper Mama rolled out a wash tub and we shelled beside the fire. Daddy bagged it and the next Saturday we all went to Judy, with faithful Ole Babe carrying two sack loads. We stopped first at the gristmill and left the corn to be ground into meal. Then we walked on up the hill to the general store and shopped for staples. If any of Daddy's fur money was left over from winter, I got a bag of stick candy and an orange.

I went bee hunting a few times with Daddy. Daddy carried an ax and a box with a screen over one end. I packed a couple of empty lard buckets. The first time we headed up into the mountain cove in back of our house, we found a little spring branch. Daddy stopped dead still and motioned me not to move. I looked to where he was pointing and saw bees sipping where the water ran over a flat rock.

A couple took off and flew into the timber. "Let's go," Daddy said. We walked as far as we could and still see the two aviators, then waited. A few minutes later we saw some more. We followed the bee line another length.

We trailed the bees to the bluff, climbed up, sighted the line again, and pursued them across the ridge to where they were all going over the opposite cliff. We got down on our stomachs and peered over the edge.

"Looky down thar," he pointed. "See 'em goin' into that ole holler red oak?"

We found a crevice and clambered down to the bee tree. He climbed the tree and chopped a hole where the bees were going in. Then he came down, got the box and the buckets, and went back up. I watched while he scooped out the honey and coaxed the bees into the box without any covering over his face. Not one single sting.

We took home almost two gallons of honey and a new hive of bees, which he shook into a new bee gum already set up by the yard fence.

Hog killin' time came after the first frost. Neighbors and relatives helped one another on Saturdays. By sunup they had a fire blazing under a big black kettle filled with cold spring water.

When the water was boiling, Daddy pulled the hog from its pen, shoved his gun barrel up close, and shot the hog square between the eyes. Two men turned the hog over while the death grunts were still rumbling in its throat, and Daddy plunged a butcher knife into the jugular. Once it was bled, they dragged it over a long, sloping flat rock. "Bring the kettle," Daddy said. They poured scalding water over the hog while Daddy and another man scraped off the skin. After a good scald, it was like slipping a loose wig off a bald man's head.

Scraped, washed, and hung, the hog was gutted and the innards tossed into Mama's galvanized wash tub (the same tub in which we shelled corn) for Mama to make lye soap. The men then washed the hulk and ripped it into shoulders, sides, and jowls. Only hair went to waste. Spare ribs, liver, heart, feet, and everything else was divided up. Everybody would have fresh meat that night.

We cousins tussled for the bladder. The victor got to push in a hollow cane and blow up the organ as big as he dared. Then we all stood around and "bomped" its taut sides until it burst. An Ozark "balloon" seldom lasted more than an hour.

The job I hated even more than hoeing corn was helping Daddy saw wood. When Daddy began sharpening his crosscut saw, I knew the time was at hand.

Usually we didn't have to cut down a tree. There were enough dead ones in the woods. By the time we were into the second log, he'd be saying, "Son, don't ride the saw. I cain't pull you and the saw both."

"Daddy, I'm t'ard."

"All right, we'll rest a minute."

We'd start again. "Son, please don't ride the saw."

We'd stop and rest.

"Son, don't ride the saw."

But he never lost his temper.

The years I spent so much time with Daddy ended in 1937 when we went to work for the WPA. I was seven years old then. I don't think he realized how important it was for me to spend time with him.

It was thirty-five years later that I got around to writing a letter of thanks for what Daddy's early companionship meant to my life.

Eleven years and eight months after I wrote the letter, Daddy was in the hospital and Mama in the nursing home. I came to visit and stayed at their house alone. Sister Freddie, who lives nearby, suggested I look in an old keepsake box for anything of my own I might want to retrieve.

I felt a little funny poking into my parents' memories, but I found the letter. It was dated April 21, 1972.

It began:

> Dear Dad,
> Knowing your birthday was coming up, I lay awake last night thinking of what I could send you. . . . I began thinking of childhood memories. As one gets older, these become very precious and meaningful, especially as they relate to one's parents. I think of our own children

who are growing up so fast and wonder what they will remember about us. We provide for them, try to keep them from danger, take them to church, pray and read the Bible, and other things. But I think they will remember little incidents where we took time with them more than some of the things we say.

In that letter he had kept so long, I recalled some of the good times—hunting, fishing, and working in the field—we had spent together during my early, formative years.

You never belittled me or made me think I was too dumb to do something. You had more patience with me than I deserved. And if I wanted to do something with you, you said, "OK, if you think you can keep up." You probably didn't realize then how much your companionship meant to me, nor what you did to build your boy's self-esteem and self-confidence.

I look around in this suburb and see a lot of kids who don't even know what their father does to earn their living. I knew what you did and we did it together.

Thanks, Dad.

FOUR
Mama Was a Teacher

You could feel a storm brewing in the thick, hot air. The chickens stopped clucking. The cat's fur stiffened as if he was preparing for a fight. Mama kept shading her eyes against the blistering sun, fretfully watching the clouds darkening and thickening over the mountain. Then the air turned suddenly chilly. Lightning streaked the sky, and thunder tumbled up and down the valley.

"Fred? Fred?" Mama called anxiously to Daddy. "It's comin' a storm. Get the lantern lit and come on to the cellar."

"I'll be thar in a minute," he answered from somewhere near the barn.

Lightning flashed and thunder broke again. A breeze stirred ever so slightly, then suddenly the wind howled, swaying the two cedars in front of the house.

"Fred, are you comin'?"

"Soon as I find my dawgs. Heah, Lion! Heah, Muse! Heah, heah, heah!"

"Forget them dogs and come get in the cellar with us!

"He always looks out for his dogs," Mama grumped as she pushed Howard Jean and me into the dark hole. The split log ceiling was just high enough for me and Brother to stand up. Mama had to hump. The walls were lined with jars of fruit and vegetables. Sweet and "I'sh" potatoes were scattered around the floor. I squished a rotten potato under a bare foot and bumped Mama. She humped back to the door and yelled again at Daddy to bring the lantern.

His face appeared in the opening. "I got Ole Muse. Cain't figure out whar' Ole Lion run off to."

"Get in here with that lantern, Fred." The rain was beginning to come down. "You're the one always talking about that cyclone that blowed lumber clear over to Cave Creek."

"Hester, that wuz 1918. Hit ain't comin' no storm now. Jist a little shower. The sky's gettin' lighter already."

That's the way it was with my parents. Every black cloud was a "cyclone" to Mama and a "little shower" for Daddy. She worried about almost everything. He seldom showed concern about anything.

Mama slaved for her family. She was the first to go help somebody who was sick. But if she had one fault it was that she was a worrier. I don't know that Daddy ever had a hearing problem, but he got to the point where he just didn't hear her, and we kids were about the same.

I believe she took her worrying after her mother, Barbara Jane Sutton Foster. Grandma Sutton came from the Red Rock community on the Other Creek. Grandma's daddy, Simon Solomon Sutton, doctored up and down that creek for over forty years until he went to a medical meeting in Little Rock and slipped and broke his leg on a banana peeling at the train station. He was crippled for the rest of his life.

Grandma Barbara had a secret that she confided to few people. As a girl, she had two ardent swains. Her doctor daddy preferred the amiable Pulliam, who always helped with chores when he visited the Suttons. "Marry the worker," Doctor Sutton urged. "The other feller won't hit a lick."

The "other feller" vowed to die if Grandma Barbara didn't marry him. After she chose Pulliam, the rejected suitor did die—whether from suicide, a disease, or an accident, Grandma never said. But Grandma always blamed herself for his death. Many thought that it contributed to her worrying so much—that and poor vision which plagued her from childhood.

Mama, the oldest of four sisters and two brothers, grew up in a log house at the head of Honey Creek, which flowed into the Other Creek. Grandpa Pulliam was away from the house much of the time, clearing new ground during the day and hunting at night. Mama and her younger sisters heard Grandma Barbara worry over all the ways their daddy could hurt himself in the woods.

Mama desperately wanted to become educated— partly, I think, because of her doctor grandpa, and partly because two of her uncles went outside and became successful lawyers. Her Uncle Taylor made a pretty good run to be lieutenant governor of Arkansas.

Her contemporaries say she was the prettiest teenager in the county. She had satiny smooth skin and wore her black hair in fashionable bangs, like the pictures in the Sears & Roebuck catalog. Her looks and her warm smile and melodic voice drew male admirers from both Big Creek and the Other Creek.

Most girls were married before sixteen. At that age Mama was boarding with her Uncle John Sutton and attending the new Southern Baptist high school academy at Parthenon in the western part of the county. She was finishing the tenth grade when the school suddenly closed for "lack of funds." It was one of many Baptist schools shut down across the South after a highly trusted church official in Atlanta stole almost a million dollars.

Mama passed the teacher's examination anyway and was assigned to the one-room Macedonia School for thirty dollars a month. She walked ten miles round trip from home to teach reading, writing, arithmetic, and grammar to about sixty kids, ages six to sixteen. Later her parents let her board with a family closer to the school.

Daddy first laid eyes on her at a picnic. She was wearing a blue cotton dress and surrounded by a circle of older young men. He was barely sixteen and she twenty, but he brashly walked over and introduced himself. A few days later she came out of school to find this lanky Hefley boy from Big Creek waiting by his horse, holding a squirrel rifle. He grinned a big hello and wondered if she'd like a ride to her boarding house.

She waited around until her pupils had left; some of the boys were as tall as Daddy. Then she rode sidesaddle behind him to the house where Daddy wangled an invitation to supper.

He began taking her regularly to pie suppers and Holiness meetings on weekends. Men in their twenties would slip around to find out which was her pie and bid on it. Daddy was then making only a quarter a day as a field hand and couldn't compete. But while another fellow might get to eat pie with her, Daddy took her home.

Mama had a mind of her own. She ignored talk that they were mismatched in age. But she told Daddy that before marriage she intended to get more schooling. She took her savings from teaching and went off to Draughon's Business College in Springfield, Missouri, a hundred miles away.

Daddy had been to the eighth grade and could write. He sent such pitiful letters that she promised to pay his tuition if he could find a place to board. He caught the next bus and boarded with his cousin, Lowell Hefley, then attending Draughon's.

After a couple of months Mama ran out of money and they both had to drop out. They were married July 16, 1928, under a big oak tree near Big Creek by JP Hope Strong. Daddy was seventeen and Mama twenty-one.

Most hillbilly marriages were not social events. A couple wanted to have the knot tied and get on with living. If they got hitched in a public ceremony, their "friends" would grab them in their wedding clothes, stuff them into a bed, and dance and whoop around the room all night. The next morning, the boys tossed the groom in the creek. Not very romantic.

Mama and Daddy moved into a "weaning house" close to where her parents lived. Wedded couples didn't take honeymoons, so the bride's parents provided a little cabin nearby where they could be alone.

Mama taught school two more years, then quit to be a full-time wife and mother. I was privileged to be her only child for almost four years.

One evening she came in from the kitchen and stood watching me play with scaly-bark hickory nuts on the hearth. Daddy was still at the barn tending to the livestock.

Stooping down beside me, she picked up a couple of nuts. "One, two, buckle my shoe," she counted. She placed two others beside them. "Three, four, shut the door. How many is two times two?"

"Four!" I squealed with satisfaction.

Then two more. "How many is three times two?"

"Six!" I yelled.

"Good boy. You are really smart. Mmmm. Give me some sugar." Smack!

Four times two. Five times. Then she repeated the process.

"OK, time to put supper on the table. We'll play this game another time."

Within a month or so I could multiply twelve by twelve. I was then barely four.

She had some dog-eared textbooks, saved from her teaching days, a reader, a geography, and a speller. She also was one of the few persons in the valley who subscribed to the weekly *Kansas City Star*.

Some weeks that was all Uncle Elmer, the mail carrier, put in our box nailed to a tree down by the creek road.

Mama spread the paper across a bed and read aloud to me the world news. I soon learned the names of President Franklin D. Roosevelt, Joseph Stalin, Madame Curie, and the brave woman flier, Amelia Earhart.

One day she read of Amelia Earhart's plans to fly solo from Hawaii to California. Four men had tried the flight and all had crashed in the ocean.

"How does an airplane keep from falling?" I asked.

She tried to explain, but I don't think she understood the principles of flight herself. Finally she said, "I don't really know how, James Carl. But one day we'll find out."

I found the word Mediterranean in the geography. "Med-i-ter-ra-ne-an." I sounded out the syllables just as she had taught me. She noticed that I said "ra" as in "rah." "No, James Carl, that's ra as in hay." I tried it again. "Good boy! Very good! Mmmmm. Now give me some sugar."

I kept saying the word, and when Daddy came in I spelled "M-e-d-i-t-e-r-r-a-n-e-a-n!" then pronounced every syllable.

Mama smiled at Daddy. "Can you spell that word, Fred?"

"Reckon not. Our boy shore is smart. I never could learn that fast." He grabbed me up and hugged me tight.

Mama tried to teach me to speak like educated people.

"You don't say, 'we'uns 'er comin','" she insisted. "You say, 'we are going.' That's the way I was taught in school."

"Shore, Mama," I piped. "We—are—going. But whar' 'bouts we'uns goin' to?"

She grinned and started all over again. After a few months I could talk pretty good around her. But when I was with my cousins, we'uns and you'uns did the goin'.

I really believed learning was easy. Mama said nothing was too hard if you worked at it long enough.

Howard Jean was born on Christmas Day, 1933. "On my birthday," Grandpa Tom said. "He'll look like me." When his hair grew out it was a light brown, but still a little like Grandpa Tom's.

When Brother got old enough to walk, he would wander into the woods if somebody wasn't looking out for him. Let him out of sight and he was digging in an ant hill or dipping his fingers in a pile of fresh horse manure. Mama would snatch him up and fuss. He'd grin as if to say, "I can't help it." She'd say, "Why can't you be like your big brother? He never gets into trouble." I'd stand there with an unholy smirk on my face.

One morning Mama left me in charge of Little Brother while she went to check the mailbox. While we were playing near the rock fence in the backyard I turned my head. When I looked back the little rascal was gone.

I feared he had crawled under the floor where Daddy had killed a big chicken snake just a week before. He wasn't there. I ran around to the bee gums. He wasn't there. I rushed to the cellar. No sign. Then I saw Mama coming and cried, "Little Brother's gone!"

She looked everywhere she could think of. "Go get your daddy out of the field." I ran as fast as my short legs could carry me. "Daddy, Daddy, Little Brother's lost!"

After an hour's more looking, Daddy was upset. He ran to get Grandpa Tom and Grandma Eller, Uncle Loma and Aunt Clara, and their little girl Ella Mae, to help. Brother wasn't in the barn, the graveyard, the corn patch, by the spring, in the orchard, or in the hollow below the house.

"I just know he got to the creek and fell in and drowned," Mama wailed.

Ella Mae came running from behind our house. "Him's sleepin' in a hen nest!"

We ran around and there he was in the pile of hay Daddy had placed on a ledge below the kitchen window. He opened his eyes and grinned as if to say, "What's all the worry about?"

A few days later I gave Mama a fright. I was walking up from Grandpa's place when I stopped to cut a fishing pole. My hand slipped and I jammed the blade of my Barlow knife into my left leg just above the knee. Mama poured turpentine and sugar into the wound and wrapped a rag around my leg to hold it in. Daddy didn't think it was that big a deal.

My injury wasn't half as bad as that of Cousin Clyde, who lived down the creek from Grandpa's place. He cut his big toe almost off while chopping down a persimmon tree. His mama poured in sugar and turpentine and tied a Bull Durham tobacco sack over it. The toe grew back crooked, as it is to this day.

Big Creek parents made do with what they had for medicines. Mama favored turpentine and sugar for wounds, fat meat poultices for croup, and Black Draught for constipation. The turpentine gagged, the poultice smelled, and the Black Draught stuck in my throat.

Mama didn't go in for skunk oil, which some folks gave their kids for throat ailments. Nor did she care for applying a juicy wad of chewing tobacco, which some said was the best remedy for snake bites. An old lady on Cave Creek mountain got bit by a rattler while plowing corn. She jerked a chew from her mouth, stuffed it in the wound, tied a rag around her foot, and went right on plowing. She lived! Mama still said chewing tobacco was nasty.

When Daddy wasn't around, I went with Mama down to the big spring by Grandpa's place where she did her washing. She carried a big sack of clothes over her back and Brother on her hip. I walked behind carrying the washboard and soap. An iron kettle and several tubs were at the spring for any woman in Grandpa Tom's family to use.

She filled the big kettle, built a fire under it, and got the water boiling hot. She scrubbed the first batch of clothes on the washboard, then wrung out each piece and pushed it in the water. Then she stood over the pot, punching the clothes with a broomstick, stirring the clothes in the water, pressing them against the bottom and sides of the kettle, sort of like a washing-machine agitator which she had never seen. All while the smoke kept watering her eyes.

When she thought she had all the dirt out, she lifted the clothes out of the big pot on the broomstick, held them up to drip, then dropped them into the rinse tub, swishing each piece in the clean water, wringing them out by hand and hanging them on a cord line stretched behind Grandpa Tom's house. Wash day took all day.

Mama still fared better than some Big Creek women. Daddy didn't ask her to plow or to hoe in the field. That was men's work, he said. He figured she had enough work to do with the house, kids, and garden. She did.

Mama's hardest time came during my fifth year. I noticed her belly swelling. She never told me what she had in there, but after observing Ole Babe, I thought I knew. Ozark women didn't discuss childbirth in mixed company. Certainly not before children. All I ever heard Mama say was that she was "in the family way."

Along after the first of February, Grandma Barbara Foster came to visit. Daddy took me and little Brother to Grandpa Tom's to be watched after by Uncle Loma and Aunt Clara who were living there then.

After getting someone to ride to Judy and summon Doc Sexton, Daddy ran back to our house to be with Mama and Grandma Foster.

Later that afternoon Doc came chugging up the creek road in his Model T. Daddy met him at the end of the lane below Grandpa Tom's. "How much do ye charge to deliver a baby?" Daddy asked.

"Fifteen for one or twenty-five for two," Doc said. "All over two are free."

"I've only got twenty saved from my fur money," Daddy admitted. "I think she may have two. She's awful big."

"I'll settle for twenty and take a chance," Doc agreed, and walked on up the hill.

Mama named the twins Betty Loucille and Mary Louise.

With Brother and the twins, she still found time to help me with my home lessons and to check my arithmetic and spelling when the babies were asleep at night. When my sixth birthday came she baked a cake for the occasion. She handed me the first piece and announced, "You're a big boy now, and next month you go to school."

School was scheduled to accommodate work needs at home. The summer term began around the first of July, after the crops were laid by, and ran until late September, when it was time to gather corn and pick cotton. The second three-month term carried through the winter months.

The morning of the big day, she dressed me in a clean denim shirt and a stiff, freshly washed pair of overalls. I picked up my pencil and the new five-cent tablet purchased on our last trip to Judy. She kissed me good-bye and I ran bouncing down the hill, skipping across Sam Cheatham's pasture, over a log laid across the creek, and up the creek road to the Holt School.

Valera Copeland, a slim, vivacious young woman in her early twenties, greeted me by name. I looked around the one-room frame building and recognized every one of my eighteen schoolmates. I had been there many times with Mama and Daddy to pie suppers and church meetings, and I felt right at home in one of the old-fashioned desks that had a shelf underneath for books and a groove on top to keep pencils from rolling off.

The lazy summer days fell into a happy routine. Miss Copeland pulled the bell rope at eight. That was the signal for "Books," meaning school is to begin. Kids came running from the school yard, which reached from the front steps to the creek. The boys sat on one side of the potbellied stove, the girls on the other. Only the teacher wore shoes.

"Grades one and two, recite!"

Six scraggly kids rushed forward and took places on a long front bench, facing Miss Copeland. As she called their names each stepped upon the low stage and read, spelled, and did numbers on the chalkboard at her directions.

After the next two grades had their turn, it was time for midmorning recess. "Girls, pass," she announced. Then, "Boys, pass." We filed quietly out, with nobody daring to let out a whoop before stepping into the yard.

Each of us brought lunch in a lard or syrup bucket, usually biscuits, a slice of ham, a sweet potato, and nuts, grapes, berries, or fruit in season. There was a bucket and dipper in the school room. Outside we drank face down from the little branch that flowed from the spring back of the school to the creek.

With only nineteen children, the teacher doubled up some of the classes. After she saw that I was advanced, she moved me to the second grade.

I attended the summer months, helped Daddy in the harvest during the fall, then returned for a winter quarter. Early in December, Miss Copeland assigned the second and third graders to draw a map of the United States and enter the name of each state and its capital. I worked long and hard by the fireplace in the evening and had it ready to take to school the next morning. About a mile up the creek I realized I had forgotten the map. I knew if I went back, I would be late for school. Then I heard a horse clomping behind me. I turned and there was Mama on Ole Babe, bringing me the map.

Just before Christmas, Mama sent a note to Miss Copeland. My teacher read it and smiled. "Your mother has invited me to come and spend the night. I'll be going home with you, James Carl. Don't leave without me."

After she rang the last bell, Miss Copeland and I stayed around to lock up. We started, with me walking a few steps in front. When we rounded a turn in the road, I spurted ahead and ducked into a thicket. When she came by, I jumped out and yelled, "Boo!" She pretended to be terrified and I ran ahead and hid again. I enjoyed this game all the way home.

Miss Copeland played with the twins while Mama cooked supper and Brother and I helped Daddy in the barn. After supper Mama and Miss Copeland talked by the fire. Miss Copeland asked her all kinds of questions, how had she done this and that when teaching. Mama asked Miss Copeland if I had been keeping up with the other second graders. "Oh, he's ahead of them all," she said. Mama grinned in pride while I pretended not to be listening.

I had only those two three-month terms with Miss Copeland. So many of the families had moved further down the creek that the Holt School was closed in 1937. I was transferred to the White House School, a mile down the creek from Grandpa's place.

Miss Copeland married and moved to Kansas City. Mama mentioned her to me many times through the years, always emphasizing, "She was your first teacher. Give her a special place in your memory."

I never saw her again until last year when I was in Kansas City visiting relatives. It had been forty-seven years and I didn't recognize the attractive woman, who looked years younger than her actual age. We sat and reminisced about my year at Holt.

She asked about Mama and I said, "She's never let me forget you. She always said you were special, since you were my first teacher."

Valera slowly shook her head. "No, James Carl. I was your second teacher. Your mama was your first, and don't you ever forget that."

I won't.

FIVE
The Valley of the Shadow

Grandma Eller Hefley lived long enough to see a car come up the creek road. "Lord, have mercy, what's that black thang down yonder?" she said. "Listen to it go put-put-put. Can't it talk plain?"

When Doc Sexton's shiny new Model T slowed to a stop, Grandma inspected it from stem to stern. Then she stepped back and gave her assessment: "Hit's back end shore does smell bad, don't it?"

Doc stopped to see her every time he came up the creek. He kept warning the family to let her get more rest. My dear wide-hipped, round-cheeked, bustling grandma was her own worst enemy. Up cooking before daylight for both people and dogs. Serving Grandpa Tom the ham he had to have three times a day. Always smiling and attentive. "Child, how ye like yer grandma's biscuits?" "Fred, ye want some more 'lasses?" "I saved the squirrel brains fer you, James Carl, since ye like 'em so well."

All day every day when I was there, it was "Grandma this," and "Grandma that." Maybe if she hadn't smiled and laughed so much, her husband and children would have realized how bad off she was. Doc said that with her heart condition she could go anytime. I guess her family found that hard to believe, since she looked so healthy.

I was home asleep when Grandma Eller died. Daddy was out coon hunting with Cousin Custer. They came back by Grandpa's place about two in the morning and noticed the lamp burning in the window. They knew something was wrong.

Somebody said she rolled off the bed, and by the time Grandpa Tom got to her she was dead. Someone else said she was on her knees praying and just fell over. One of my older cousins claimed she was sitting on the chamber pot when she passed on to her reward. However she went, she died at fifty-seven, having raised eleven healthy children and birthed dead triplets.

The men dug the grave and made the coffin. The women washed and dressed her diseased body, straightening the worn out legs, tying the puffy ankles, crossing the arms and tying them across the chest. When she got stiff, she was straight as a hickory sapling. Other women made the burial dress and tacked cambric lined with lace around the top of her coffin. Still others brought heaps of food. All while we younger cousins played games in the meadow, not knowing enough to be solemn.

With no embalming for the body, Big Creek folks couldn't wait for distant kinfolks to come. By the time the body was washed, dressed and lifted into the homemade pine coffin, kin and neighbors from close by had gathered for the funeral at the house.

Grandpa Tom, his russet hair neatly combed and moustache waxed, sat stiffly in a straight hickory chair beside the coffin. His large family filled the porch protectively around him, with neighbors spilling into the yard.

"Uncle" Dan Hefley was the preacher. He wasn't really my uncle. He and his three brothers had moved to Big Creek around the turn of the century from Marble Falls in the northern part of the county. If there was any connection to my Harv Hefley clan, nobody knew about it then. This tall, lanky, stoop-shouldered, double-jointed preacher was simply everybody's Uncle Dan.

Uncle Dan was a Holiness farmer-preacher. He and Grandpa Tom were miles apart on biblical doctrines. Grandpa didn't believe in a "second blessing," divine healing, speaking in tongues, and foot washing, as Uncle Dan did. But he and Dan were longtime friends and coon-hunting partners.

"Reckon everybody's hyar that's a comin'," Uncle Dan announced. "We'll start the sangin'. Everybody jine in."

"We . . . read . . . of . . . a . . . place . . . that's . . . called . . . heaven. . . ."

Uncle Dan sounded the first line ever so slowly, giving everybody time to pick up the tune.

> . . . *Hit's made for the pure and the free.* . . . .
> *Fair haven of rest fer the weary,*
> *How beautiful heaven must be.*

Uncle Dan knew these were Church of Christ Hefleys. He didn't jump and clap in celebration as he did at the homegoing of a Pentecostal saint. In respect to the family, he read quietly from the Bible, even holding back on his usual "Praise the Lords" and "Amens."

"We all know that Eller wuz a good womern, who knowed the Lord and loved to sarve him. She wuz a faithful wife to Brother Tom hyar, and de-voted to her many chillern and grandchillern. She never let on how much she suffered, but accordin' to Doc, she wuz in pain a lot."

Grandpa sat solemnly nodding his head. I hung close to Daddy, who was wearing a white shirt and necktie and trying hard not to cry.

"We mourn for Sister Eller because we loved her and wanted her to stay a little longer. But the dear Lord didn't see it that way. He said 'Eller, hit's 'bout time ye were comin' Home. We need ye up hyar. Yes, we need ye up hyar. To sang with the angels.' Oh, hallelujah, people! I'm sorrowful and I'm happy, cuz I know this dear saint is with the Lord and the angels.

"Brother Tom and sons and daughters, this pore ole sick body hyar ain't yer loved one. This is jist the ole shell she cast off when the Lord said, 'Come up yander.' Her spirit's with the Lord, in that sweet home of the happy and free. Oh hallelujah, ain't it wunnerful!"

You could see a few smiles amid the tears, like the sun trying to break through a dark cloud that had hovered over the old house all day. Everybody said there was no one like Uncle Dan when it came to preaching funerals. You might not approve of his jumping around and hollering hallelujah in meetings, but you couldn't argue against the sunshine he brought when your loved one was gone.

Uncle Dan read off the list of survivors which had been given him: sister Fanny, "gone to Texas with her seventeen young'uns"; brother Pink, also in Texas; Ma and Pa deceased "since Eller wuz a little girl, leavin' her to Aunt Delly Davis and Aunt Sary Greenhaw to take care of." He mentioned Grandpa Tom, the children, and "more grandchillern, I reckon, than any of us kin name."

He gave a prayer, then six men picked up the pine coffin and started the long walk up the narrow trail to the graveyard. Grandpa Tom walked behind the coffin, head bent, lips quivering, family and neighbors following.

The pallbearers entered the wire gate, walked past Grandpa Jim's tombstone, and set the coffin down beside the yawning, freshly dug hole in the clay.

"Gather 'round, folks," Uncle Dan said. He read some verses, then the casket lid was lifted so we could have one last look.

Oh, the wailing when the coffin lid was lifted for the last time! The crying and taking on, with poor Grandpa Tom standing by Grandma's coffin, accepting tearful hugs and condolences. It was that way at every funeral, especially at the graveside. Kinfolks and neighbors expressed their feelings openly and didn't worry about what somebody else might think. Forgotten for the moment were old spites, hurt feelings, and even differences over religious doctrines.

There was unity beside a loved one's death.

The coffin lid was closed and nailed tight. They sang "The Uncloudy Day," a standard at Ozark funerals. "Dust thou art and unto dust thou shalt return," intoned Uncle Dan. The men slowly lowered the coffin on plow lines into the hole. Then they jerked the lines free. I heard the first shovel of dirt hit the coffin.

Daddy pulled me away. "We'll see Grandma Eller again," he said huskily. "That's our hope."

Grandma Bett went next, and the yard in front of the old house was again crowded for a funeral. The menfolks carried her long coffin up the same steep trail and lowered her into a hole beside Grandpa Jim.

I was seven when she died, and was puzzling over what happened to dead people. Uncle Dan said when you breathed your last breath, your spirit went to be with the Lord. But there was coming a resurrection morning when the dead people would break open their coffins and rise to meet the Lord in the air. One of my uncles said dead people just rotted away like animals. I had seen dead animals in all stages of deterioration. I remembered the wildcat that had broken out of the corn crib and the skeleton I had found near the spring. Would my grandparents remains look like that? Would their skeletons come back to life and rejoin their spirits in heaven?

The grownups sang at meetings in the school house:

> *There's a great day coming,*
> *A great day coming,*
> *There's a great day coming by and by*

When the saints and the sinners
Shall be parted right and left. . . .

Uncle Willie Pink said that on Judgment Day the Lord and the devil would go through the graveyards, with the Lord pointing and saying, "You take this 'un, and I'll take that 'un."

I dreamed of being in the graveyard on Judgment Day. I saw two ghostly figures, the Lord and the devil, walking among the tombstones. I heard the Lord saying, "You take this one and I'll take that 'un. . . ." I saw them coming for me. "Mama, Mama," I yelled, thrashing under the covers. "Don't let the devil take me."

"Go back to sleep, James Carl," she said reassuringly from the next bed. "Nothing's going to hurt you." Daddy just kept snoring away.

I heard Uncle Dan say, "Ole Death comes to ever'body, the young'uns and the old 'uns. Ye young-'uns who think yer gonna live fer'ever, go up to the graveyard and measure the graves with a string. Ye'll find yer size thar."

I didn't have to do that. Every time I went by the graveyard, I saw the little houses built over Albert and Dennis' graves. Children did die.

This was when Daddy was working on the WPA. He left before daylight, riding Ole Babe six or seven miles, past Judy to where they were cutting an all-weather road up Cave Creek Mountain. He got back just in time to milk and feed the livestock. Most nights he was too tired to go hunting. I didn't see much of my daddy and I didn't like it.

Uncle Loma and Aunt Clara were still living with Grandpa Tom, who was seldom home. I heard that Grandpa was out looking for a new wife. I was sure he'd never find one to beat Grandma Eller.

Grandpa attended all the special events at Judy, Church of Christ meetings and debates, and especially singing schools where they followed the shaped note Stamps-Baxter song books. He was sitting in the Judy school house one Saturday, watching the teacher direct a new song, when his glasses fell to the floor. Those around him thought he tumbled to the floor while trying to retrieve his glasses.

Then someone shouted, "Tom, Tom, air ye sick?"

"Git Doc Sexton! Hurry! He's out lak a lite."

Doc came running with his little black bag and examined him there in the school house. "I think he's been struck with paralysis," Doc said. "Carry him down to Lloyd's."

Lloyd, Grandpa's nephew, had a post office and store building just below the school house. Doc kept Grandpa there awhile, then moved him into a house for a few days. "Ain't no more we can do fer him here," Doc finally told the family. "Might as well take him back up the creek to his own house." His sons carried him home in a wagon.

I saw him propped up in bed, unable to talk or play his fiddle. The old black cat that he loved so much jumped on the bed and fell asleep beside him. Grandpa looked at the cat, then at his fiddle, and great big tears rolled down his cheeks. He made funny noises, like a baby trying to talk. It was so pitiful.

We came to keep him company. His daughters brought food and he ate pretty well. The men talked about coon hunting, hoping to cheer him up.

One evening we finished supper and moved into the front room to be near the fire. Grandpa Tom was lying on his bed, listening, making a gurgle now and then, as if he wanted to tell us something. Of course he couldn't.

Somebody struck up a gospel tune,

> *Now let us have a little talk with Jesus,*
> *Let us tell 'em all about our troubles,*
> *He will har air faintest cry . . . and*
> *He will answer by and by.*

Everybody turned in surprise to see Grandpa moving his lips.

"Pa's a sangin' with us!" one of his sons declared in amazement. Grandpa *was* singing and smiling. But when the singing stopped, Grandpa stopped. He tried to talk and couldn't. Singing and seeing his family gathered about were the last joys he had on earth.

Daddy was plowing in the cornfield when the messenger came to our house to report Grandpa Tom had died. "Go call your daddy," Mama said.

When I reached him I blurted it out: "Grandpa Tom is dead."

Daddy said only, "OK, Son," as if he had been expecting it, and walked silently with me to the house.

Grandpa was sixty-seven years old. Uncle Dan preached the funeral. I didn't cry. I don't recall any particular strong feelings as I looked at my grandfather, wearing a coat and tie and looking like a judge in the pine coffin.

Grandpa wasn't a bad man. He loved all of us in his own way, and we loved him. But we just didn't feel great affection for him.

Cousin Emma and I were talking about this recently. "We can't erase our memories," she said, "but we can be selective in what we dwell on. I try to see Grandpa not when he was fussing at us, but when he was playing his fiddle in the family circle. He looked so kind and loving and tranquil then. That's the Grandpa I try to think about."

Cousin Emma has three brothers—Ernest, Glenn, and Jimmy John. She and I are about the same age and Glenn is a little older. I felt closer to them, when we were growing up on Big Creek, because of sharing their sorrow when their mother died.

Their daddy was the storyteller, Uncle Willie Pink; their sickly mama was Aunt Blanche, whom Uncle Willie met and married while he was picking cotton on her daddy's farm in Oklahoma.

Uncle Willie brought Aunt Blanche, Glenn and Emma's mama, to live in a ramshackle house at the edge of a pasture, over a mile from the nearest neighbor. Aunt Blanche was never happy there. Her father offered to provide them a house and land if they'd return to Oklahoma. She wanted to go badly, but Uncle Willie always said, "We'd starve to death on the way back out thar." So they stayed put, because men on Big Creek always had their way.

I loved to visit them. Nobody on Big Creek could cook as fancy and as tasty as Aunt Blanche. And nobody could tell stories like Uncle Willie Pink.

At night we'd sit on their porch looking up at the stars and Sam's Throne, which stuck up on the side of the mountain like a giant knob above their house. Ringed by a bluff with about a two-acre summit of trees, Sam's Throne was the most intriguing and mysterious place of my childhood. I never tired of hearing Uncle Willie tell the story.

"This hyar feller Sam Davis cum in hyar around a hundert y'ars ago. He wuz lookin' for his sister who had been captured by Injuns back in Tennessee. He had jist about give out all hope, when one day he wuz cow huntin' on Cave Creek and heard a familyar voice in the woods. It wuz his long lost sister.

"W'al, they had a joyful reuniting and she took him to meet her husband, a Choctaw Injun chief. That chief he took a likin' to ole Sam and gave him this land down on the creek which we call the Davis Farm. Back then it included our place and reached all the way to the Throne.

"Ole Sam was a powerful b'ar and buffalo hunter. With that and cattle tradin', he made a pile of money and owned a bunch of slaves before the Civil War. After the war his son Dick wuz kilt—to settle an ole war feud, I've heerd. W'al, Ole Sam jist went plumb crazy after that. He found a crack in the bluff through which he could climb to the top of the little mountain. He went up thar and built himself a little house and put boards over the crack to keep the b'ars and wildcats out. Finally, his family had to go up after 'em and bring 'em back down.

"Now ole Sam, as I told ye, made a heap of money. He put his gold money in a little holler cedar log and packed it up on the little mountain and hid it. His family brought him back down, but he'd go right back up thar, sometimes stayin' for days.

"Ole Sam was a preacher of sorts. He'd git on that bluff and holler, 'Repent! Repent! Jedgment is a comin'!' On a clear still day, they say, he could be heerd plumb down to the creek. That's when they started callin' it Sam's Throne."

At this point I knew Uncle Willie was coming to the most exciting part. He'd fill his pipe and try to light it, while we sat around him, begging him to get back on the story.

"W'al now, ole Sam said the Lord tolt him he wuz gonna live a thousand years and keep preachin' until everybody on Big Creek repented and got ready for the Jedgment Day. W'al folks don't know how long he lived, cuz his family went up thar to git him and he wuz gone. They couldn't find hide ner hair of the ole feller.

"Nobody ever found his skeleton, 'er the money 'er anythang. Plenty have looked, especially fer his money. They've dug up the whole top of the Throne lookin'. Nobody's ever found it."

One of us always asked, "Do you think his gold is still up thar?"

"Shore, ain't no reason to think not. Course, animals could have drug his body off. That's my thanking. But animals wouldn't have no use fer gold."

Uncle Willie always closed by warning, "Don't ye young'uns thank of goin' up on that ole Throne. Ye could fall off that bluff and kill yerself. Don't let me catch ye anywhar close, y'hyar?"

We'd promise, and the next day Glenn and Emma and I would walk up to the bluff and dare one another to go through the crack. "I ain't a'goin'," Glenn said. "Pa'll lick the tar out of me."

It was at this time when their mother was so sick. We could see the pain in her watery eyes and the ugly running sores on her legs. We couldn't see her diseased kidneys. She may also have had cancer.

Aunt Blanche died the same year as Grandpa Tom. She was only thirty-four, just a little older than Mama.

Clara Kent, the school teacher, made her a white burial dress. They brought her down the mountain in a pine box to the Hefley graveyard. When they opened the box at the grave we could still see the print of the quarters on her eyelids which had been used to keep her eyes from popping open.

I looked over and saw Glenn and Emma crying. Losing their mama was almost more than they could bear. There was Uncle Willie looking bewildered and lost. For once he didn't have a story.

I hurt and quivered all over and was afraid. Mama was standing right by me, crying, and holding our new baby, Jimmie Fern. The twins, Louise and Loucille, were hanging onto Mama's legs, while Brother was poking at the grave dirt with a stick.

It was a dark and dreary day and clouds shrouded the mountain behind us and hid Sam's Throne. They sang, "The Uncloudy Day"; the preacher said his final piece; and they lowered the coffin. "Yer mama's gone, let's go home," Uncle Willie said to my cousins.

"Fred, help me get these kids down to the house," Mama said. Daddy motioned for me to come on. We trudged down the hill toward our log house, Daddy leading the way and me trailing behind with Brother. I kept thinking: *Suppose that had been our mama in that pine box. Suppose Daddy had been taking us home without her.*

"Mama, you won't die and leave us?" I implored.

Mama looked back at me in attempted reassurance. "'Course not. Now stop thinking such a terrible thing."

Grandpa Tom and Aunt Blanche were the last ones buried in our family cemetery. I was nine years old then and deeply troubled about death. Grandpa Jim, Grandma Bett, Grandma Eller, and Grandpa Tom had all died in the 1930s and were resting beneath the cold ground in our graveyard. But old folks dying was one thing. Glenn and Emma's mother was another. The little houses over Albert and Dennis' graves were always a reminder that kids died, too. Whatever death was, wherever the loved ones went, death didn't seem fair.

The years marched away. I grew up and had my own family. I have seen many more loved ones and friends die, walked in many graveyards and stood before many tombs, gazed at the eternal flame which burns for the Kennedy brothers in Arlington Cemetery. I have entered the dazzling, white marbled Taj Mahal in India, twenty-one years in building by 20,000 servants for Shah Jhan's favorite wife.

I returned last year to the little graveyard on the hill. It was early December and a chill was in the damp air. My brother, Howard Jean, was with me.

I was fifty-three and he almost fifty. We made our way through the briars and high grass to the graves of our long dead loved ones. We could plainly read the lettering on Grandpa Jim and Grandma Bett's big stone; the hand-etched markings on Grandpa Tom and Grandma Eller's rocks (plucked from the hillside) were harder to make out. The little houses I remembered so well over Albert and Dennis' graves were gone. But there was a new stone for Aunt Blanche, placed there by her children and simply inscribed MOTHER.

"Think anything's left down there?" Howard asked, pointing to the ground.

"You mean, of the bodies? I guess they're just skeletons by now."

"That's all?"

"Maybe coffin nails, buttons, and some of the material from their burial clothes."

My brother looked somber as he peered at the stones of his grandparents. "Were they important people?"

"Here in the valley, they were well known. Outside, they had a few kinfolks who didn't have time to get to the funeral. I guess that's about all."

I looked at the familiar words below Grandpa Jim's date of death: GONE BUT NOT FORGOTTEN. "They'll be remembered a long time," I said. "And we'll see them in heaven, I hope."

We scuffed around some more, two brothers lost in thoughts and dim memories of the long ago.

I looked out toward the eastern mountain and saw the familiar landmark of Sam's Throne, half-covered by cloud. I wondered about Sam Davis. What had really happened to him? Where were his remains? The old man of the valley, the biggest landowner, now alive only in legend.

Howard glanced at his watch. "We'd better leave if we're aimin' to get back before dark."

Turning to walk away, I suddenly remembered the last song sung at Aunt Blanche's funeral. The words came rushing back, words we had clung to in time of death:

> *O they tell me of a home far beyond the skies*
> *O they tell me of a land far away*
> *O they tell me that he smiles on his children thar*
> *O the land of the uncloudy day . . .*

That'll be the day!

SIX
Basics at the White House

When you said "White House" anybody on Big Creek knew you weren't talking about President Roosevelt's residence, but a place far more important to us—the little one-room white clapboard building that served as school, community center, and church. Great-grandpa Jim, Grandpa Tom, Daddy, and I all went to the school a mile down the creek from Grandpa's place. I started in July 1937, after my two three-month terms at Holt.

Half the fun was getting there. I joined a pack of cousins at Grandpa's place. We went trooping down the road, splashing barefooted through the creek, then racing for the big mulberry tree just before the road turned at the Joe Reddell place.

At the mulberry tree we had a choice of taking the road—the long way around, or cutting across Reddell's field—the short way. The problem with the shorter route was a threatening herd of goats, led by a monstrous billy with horns like a steer.

One warm summer morning we were perched in the mulberry tree, like so many monkeys, munching berries and eyeing the goats. Billy Buck, Aunt Alda's son, pointed to the old billy nibbling grass just over the barbed wire fence. "I'll bet you can't outrun 'em this morning," he challenged.

"Aw, I can run faster than that ole goat," I said as if it were no big deal.

"And I'll bet you cain't."

"Watch me. I'll be halfway across the field 'fore he even knows what's goin' on."

I jumped down from the limb where I had been sitting and slipped quietly to the fence. Casting a sideward glance to see that the goat was still occupied, I put one bare foot in the wire, glanced at the goat again, then swung over the top and started running.

Halfway across the field, I heard Billy Buck scream, "That ole goat's a comin' atter ye!"

I didn't dare look back. I just kept hoofing it, my eyes on the far fence and safety.

"Maaaaaaaa! Maaaaaaa!" The ole billy was coming up fast. "Maaaaaaa! Maaaaaaa!" I could almost feel his breath on my neck. There was the fence. My only chance was to jump. I leaped. Rip! Rip! "Maaaaaa! Maaaaaa!" I caught the seat of my overalls on the fence, but momentum carried me over. I landed face down and jumped up to find the goat leering from the other side.

"Maaaaa yerself, you ole billy! I beatcha this time. Ha, ha, ha!"

A cool breeze blew between my bare legs. I felt cautiously behind. The rip in the denim ran from my waist to the back of one knee. The only good thing was that the wire had left only a red streak on my flesh.

Billy Buck and the three Reddell boys—Kenneth, Johnny Lee, and Robert—caught up. They were all giggling, which didn't help my dignity at all. "Whatta ya got yer hands behind yer back fer?" Billy Buck smirked.

"I ripped my britches on the fence."

"I'll get one of the girls at school to sew 'em up."

"No thanks, I'll make out."

"Ya gonna hold yerself that way all day?"

"I'll stay at my desk."

"Suit yerself," my cousin said and went running ahead with his giggling companions.

I dragged into school just as the bell rang, and edged into my desk without anyone else noticing my predicament. At recess Clara Kent wanted to know why I wasn't going out to play.

"I don't feel well, Mrs. Kent."

"You want to lie down in the corner?"

"No, ma'am. I think I'll just stay here."

Mrs. Kent knew children pretty well. "Did you mess in your britches on the way to school?"

I blushed all colors. "No, ma'am, but, well"—I knew I might as well tell the truth—"I ripped my seat on a fence. Running from the Reddell's ole billy goat."

She laughed. "I've got needles and thread and can fix you until you get home to your mama. Come on, stand up. I won't tell anybody."

"Billy Buck and the Reddell boys know. They're already tellin' everybody."

"Forget them. Now stand up so I can take care of it."

While I kept an eye on the door, she sewed up the rip. "That didn't take long, did it? Now go on out and play. If they tease you, tease right back."

I skittered happily for the door, ready again to face the world.

Cousin Glenn now says reverently of this woman, who later made his mama's burial dress, "Clara Kent probably touched more kids' lives on Big Creek than anybody else. She was both a teacher and a second mama to all of us."

Clara, a bright-eyed, red-haired young woman who attended Arkansas Tech between terms at the White House, was a Strong, married to Howard Kent, and living with his parents on the lower part of the old Sam Davis Farm. Clara knew Mama very well. She and sisters Niva and Opal Strong attended the Baptist Academy at Parthenon before it closed, then went on to Central Baptist College at Conway, Arkansas.

Their father, John Strong, was much criticized for sacrificing to send his girls to college "when all they'll do is come back and get married."

"W'al," he said, "if they cain't take care of me when I'm old, maybe they'll have enough pull to git me in the poor house." All three became teachers, but Clara was the one I knew best. She was my teacher at the White House from the third to the eighth grade.

The White House was probably the first building to get a coat of white paint on upper Big Creek, thus the name. The little frame structure fronted on the rocky, rutted road which ran along the high bank overlooking our school swimming hole. Drinking water was carried from a spring flowing from under a small bluff on the hill. We all gulped from the same dipper.

We washed our hands in the branch that ran beside the school, dried them on our shirttails, and ate lunch under scalybark hickory nut trees near the creek. We played all over the hillside, behind the school, and in the meadow across the creek. During high water, we crossed on a narrow swinging board footbridge that ran on cables suspended thirty feet above the water from the high bank on one side to the fork of an oak on the other. At recess and lunch hour there were always two or three boys bouncing on the boards, or hanging from the cables, rocking the bridge, and daring any girl to cross.

Clara started the school day by reading a Bible passage, as then required by Arkansas law. She divided her fifty some children into learning groups, and had one group at a time come to the front and recite. While this was happening, she had more advanced students teaching the others.

I was only seven, but she quickly put me in the third and fourth grade group. She also made me an "assistant teacher" to drill the first and second graders.

As at Holt, the White House had two three-month terms during a year, scheduled so the children could help with crops. Clara promoted me every term, and

I was thus able to reach the eighth grade in three years. She promoted and demoted, made her own rules, and answered only to the local board, which to my recollection never looked in while school was in session.

Clara believed in competition, and may the best pupil win. She put everything aside on Friday afternoon for the weekly ciphering match and spelling bee.

In ciphering it was one on one with the winner staying up the longest. She started with the lowest grades, giving them easy numbers, and ended with seventh and eighth graders doing cube roots and hard fractions.

During my second year, my biggest competitor was a girl we called Big Geraldine, sixteen, and weighing at least two hundred and fifty pounds. We made a laughable looking pair, Big Geraldine in her long sweeping dress beside this skinny little black-haired boy whose head reached only to her waist.

"OK," Clara would say. "Farmer Brown earned three-fifths of a dollar and sixty cents for a day's work, and saved three-eighths of this amount. How much did he save? Ready? Set! Go!"

And the chalk would fly.

By my third year, I was the last one standing almost every Friday.

For spelling, Clara appointed two captains and had them choose up sides. Everybody, from first to eighth grades, got chosen. Then we spelled from one side to another. When a player on one side missed, the word went to someone on the other side. If he spelled it correctly, his side got a point. The team earning the most points won.

Our teacher was called Mrs. Kent in school and Clara outside. She played Dare Base with the big kids, Drop the Handkerchief with the smaller ones, and Kick the Can and Auntie Over with everyone. She did not play Fox and Dog, in which we ranged all over the hillside and across the creek. When time came for "Books," she wanted to be close by the school to ring the bell.

In school she was all business. We knew there was a wooden paddle behind her desk and we could see the hickory limb that hung on the back wall between the two blackboards.

One morning I kept pursing my lips, blowing out only air, until suddenly I blurted out a shrill whistle. She whirled around from writing a sentence on the blackboard and demanded, "Who's trying to be funny?"

I didn't look up, keeping my head over the fractions on my nickel tablet. Big Geraldine tittered behind me.

"Whoever it was, I'd better not hear it again."

When she turned back to her work I caught the dare in Billy Buck's eye. I pursed my lips again and—"tweeeeeet!"

This time she caught me.

"Come forward, James Carl." I saw her take down the hickory limb.

I got up slowly, dragging my feet.

"Move it!"

Big Geraldine laughed out loud. Billy Buck, and Cousin Glenn, and several others were snickering.

"That's enough. I'd better not hear a sound from anybody else."

I stood before her in the awful moment. "Raise your britches' legs to your knees," she ordered.

I obeyed. "Thwack! Thwack! Thwack!" I grimaced and gritted my teeth to keep from crying out as the limb stung the naked flesh.

"Go back to your seat. If you do it again, you'll get twice the dose I gave you."

I never whistled again during Books.

One of Clara's complaints was the tobacco stains left around the stove after a community meeting the night before. "I wish these men could learn to aim their spit," she'd say.

She knew some of the older boys chewed tobacco. She couldn't always be checking their mouths, but she could forbid them to spit in the school house. "If you have to spit," she said, "raise your hand and I'll excuse you to go outside."

One morning one of the older girls came to her complaining that little Andy, about seven, had been spitting tobacco juice on the floor. Clara walked back to his seat and there was the evidence, plain to see.

"You do that again and I'll spank you hard," she threatened.

After the noon recess the same girl came back. "It's little Andy," she said.

Clara reached for her paddle. "I warned him."

"Wait, Mrs. Kent, he's stopped spitting on the floor."

"Well, good—now what about him?"

"He's spitting down his overalls."

Mama had talked to me plenty about chewing tobacco and smoking roll-your-owns. When Zeke Hamilton, an older boy, offered me a chew, I said, "No, thanks. Mama says it's a dirty habit."

"She did, huh. W'al, ye need to see how it tastes, Mama's Boy." He called to another boy, "Hey, Horace. Mama's Boy wants a taste of chawin' terbaccer."

Zeke grabbed me around the neck. "Hold his mouth open 'n give 'em a wad of yer good stuff."

I bit down hard on Horace's fingers. "Ye do that agin and I'll knock the stuffin' out of ye," he warned.

He pushed the wad behind my tongue and jerked his hand out before I could bite down. I gagged, choked, coughed, and turned green.

"Ye tell Clary and we'll give you some more on the way home," Zeke shouted.

I didn't dare breathe a word. I also never had the desire to taste tobacco again in any form.

Clara knew the families on Big Creek who wanted their children to get educated and those who didn't care whether they went to school or not. If I didn't show up, she knew I was really sick for Mama to keep me home. I seldom missed.

One morning Joey, about twelve, came into the school house crying. Clara knew that his mother had died recently and thought he was still grieving. "No'm, I'm gettin' over that," he said. "Hit's Pa. He says bein' Mama's gone, he needs me to help out at home. He says, I don't need no book larnin' to plow corn. He tolt me to tell ye that so ye'd understand why I won't be comin' back."

Clara knew the family lived far back up in a mountain cove, and that the father could barely read and write. She also knew how much he loved his children.

"You really want to get an education?" she asked the disconsolate boy.

"Oh, yes'um. I want to so bad hit hurts. But Pa, he jist thinks I should be home helpin' him."

"Have you been helping him after school?"

"Oh, yes'um, and on Saturdays and Sundays, too. I can plow as well as he kin."

"Have you tried crying?" Clara asked.

"Cryin'? What fer?"

"To make your pa see how bad you want to go to school."

"Pa don't like me to cry. He says, hit makes 'em feel orful."

"Well, you try it awhile. Maybe that will work."

"Yes'um, I will. Thank ye, Miz Kent. Thank ye."

Joey was in school the next day, and the next. That evening, at a community function, Joey's father pulled Clara aside. "Clary, I cain't do a thang with that boy of mine. He jist cries and bawls to go to school. I reckon I'll have to let him come. I cain't stand any more of his takin' on."

"I understand," Clara said. "I know how much of a sacrifice it is for you. But school will be out pretty soon and he can help you full time in the field."

"Yes'm, I'm counting on that. R'at now, I reckon, I'll jist have to let 'em go to school."

I also saw Clara some Sundays at the interdenominational Sunday school at the White House where she was one of the teachers. Having little kids, Mama couldn't go much herself. But she tried to see that I got there.

Clara gave each of her Sunday school pupils Bible picture cards which she ordered from the David C. Cook Publishing Company in Illinois. I took my cards home and showed them to Mama and we talked about the Scripture verses printed on them.

One Sunday there was a car at the White House. Often we didn't see a car for weeks and weeks, and here was a shiny new Model A with an Illinois license tag. When I went inside Clara introduced me to two well-dressed ladies. "This is Miss Florence Billings and Miss Marie Olsen," she said. "They are missionaries from the Moody Bible Institute in Illinois. That's close to where we get the picture cards." Then to the ladies: "Florence and Marie, this is the boy I was telling you about."

Miss Billings and Miss Olsen came every month to teach the whole Sunday school. Miss Olsen put pictures on a flannel board to illustrate her Bible stories. I was enthralled and could hardly wait for the next month when they would come again.

Christmas was the most special time of year at the White House. Like most Big Creek families, we didn't do much celebrating at home. Mama propped up a little cedar in a corner of the house. She showed Howard Jean and me how to string popcorn around the tree. She encouraged me to write letters to Santa Claus. We got an orange a piece, maybe a stick of candy, and if Daddy got a good price for his fur, a more special present such as a twenty-five-cent Barlow knife.

Early in December Clara dropped our names in a cap and shook it several times. As she called our names, each of us came forward and pulled out a slip of paper. The name written on it was the person we were to buy a present for. The rule was that we couldn't spend more than a quarter and we couldn't tell anyone what we had bought.

Around the tenth of the month five or six older boys took an ax and crossed the swinging bridge to cut down the Christmas tree. The prettiest, fullest, and tallest cedars grew on that ·side of the creek. They came dragging the tree back, with the rest of us whooping and hollering alongside, and Clara telling us to stay out of their way. Once the tree was placed on the stage, everybody joined in the decorating. We ran 'round and 'round the tree with our strings of popcorn, with the taller kids standing on desks to reach the top. Then we made red and green tissue paper chains, which we also strung on the tree.

The decoration accomplished, we began rehearsing the Christmas "play," which was really just a string of spoken poems and recitations on a theme. Every one of us had a part, which had to be learned by heart. Day after day Clara sat by the stage, prompting, correcting, encouraging us on, hugging the younger ones when they got their parts "exactly right."

The big day, Friday before Christmas, Mama raked my scalp with her fine-tooth comb, something she didn't do every day. "I don't want you to stand up there and have everybody see a big louse come crawling down your face," she said.

"Ouch, ouch!" I yelled. "Mama, you're drawin' blood! Mama, that's enough!"

With that ordeal over, Mama gave me clean overalls and shirt and sent me off to school with the ten-cent bracelet Daddy had bought at Judy for the girl whose name I had drawn.

I carried enough food for dinner and supper, for I wouldn't be coming home before the program. We practiced and sang carols all day. At four o'clock, the usual time of dismissal, Clara gave us a recess while she checked to see that everything was just right. The tree was up and decorated, the presents wrapped and under it. The stage curtain—an old white bed sheet sewn to a colored spread—was strung across the front. The Nativity scene was in place—just two boards over a couple of saw horses with a doll for Baby Jesus resting in a clump of hay. When the school was swept clean and the floor around the stove scrubbed clean of tobacco juice stains, all was ready.

Clara rang the bell and we came rushing back for the dress rehearsal. "Mary" wore a long dress and a flour sack tied over the back of her head. The rest of the "players" wore regular clothes.

Our parents started coming around six, walking, on horseback, and some in spring wagons. The men put their lanterns in the window and put extra wood on the fire, then went back to sit with their wives and babies. The cast—every student in the school—fidgeted two and three to a desk near the front, waiting expectantly.

The magic moment came. Clara stood up in front and smiled at everybody. She gave a welcome and expressed her pride in us. She led everybody in several Christmas carols accompanied by a couple of guitars. Then two older boys pulled back the curtains, displaying the manger and the tree with the presents underneath. The show was ready to begin.

One by one we said our pieces. This Christmas mine was a long poem about a Christmas star, guiding the wise men to Bethlehem. I saw Mama and Daddy straining to hear with Howard Jean squirming in the crook of Daddy's arm. The twins snoozed on a pallet and Mama held our new baby, Jimmie Fern, as she grinned with pride. All around the room were uncles and aunts, older cousins, and neighbors. I knew everybody in that room and they knew me. On center stage, proud and assured, I spoke my part without missing a word.

The last speaker sat down and Santa Claus—Uncle Loma—burst into the room, carrying a bulging sack over his shoulders.

"Ho! Ho! Ho!" Stepping over sleeping babies, he wove his way to the front and put down the sack.

"Have ye'all been good boys and girls?"

"Yeaahhhh!" we screamed back.

"Well, I've got some presents for ye." He opened the sack and began passing out oranges and little brown bags of peppermint stick candy to each of us.

"Ho! Ho! Ho! Looky hyar under the tree." He picked up the first present and called a name. I waited just as eagerly to see the girl open my present as I did to receive my own, a shiny new "french harp," what outsiders would call a harmonica.

The last gift was given out, the final carol sung, the prayer of benediction offered by Uncle Dan Hefley. Grown-ups stood around talking while we children ran around the room shouting, "Looky what I got!"

"Come on, Son," Daddy called. "Your mama wants to git the little 'uns home."

Carrying my treasures, I scooped up my sister Loucille. Daddy took the other twin, Mama packed the baby, and Brother came trudging behind, carrying his orange and bag of candy. Daddy helped Mama onto Ole Babe and handed up Jimmie Fern, then put a twin in front and a twin behind. He walked in front, holding the lantern and leading the horse, with Howard and me skipping alongside.

Ahead and behind us in the freezing darkness we could see the yellow glow of lanterns guiding others home. The stars shone above us and owls hooted from the woods on either side. Peace on earth and good will to all in Big Creek Valley.

That was my last Christmas at the White House School, my last term under Clara Kent. She and her husband moved to Missouri, where she completed both her Bachelor's and Master's degrees. I saw her only three or four times during the next forty-four years.

On my last trip to the Ozarks, I heard Clara and Howard had retired and moved back to Arkansas, living near the Jasper-Harrison highway. I decided to visit.

When I arrived they were gathered with some strangers around a construction site on adjoining property. Clara introduced me to her niece, Pauline, and Pauline's husband, Walt. Pauline and I had been classmates at the White House.

"This will be their house," Clara said. "We're just about to have the ceremony for the laying of the cornerstone. Would you join with us as our special guest?" she invited.

Walt gave a prayer, then Pauline read from a worn Bible. "Go up to the mountain, and bring wood, and build the house; and I will take pleasure in it, and I will be glorified, saith the Lord. . . . Except the Lord build the house, they labor in vain that build it."

"This Bible was given to me in June 1936 by my Aunt Clara Kent for memorizing Bible verses in Sunday school," Pauline said. She added a brief family history and handed the Bible to Walt for placing in the cornerstone. Clara read a poem she had written for the occasion and asked me to give a closing prayer.

"Let's go up to the house and visit awhile," Clara said. I walked along beside this still beautiful woman in her sixties. I thought of another foundation, the one she had helped lay for my life.

We chatted an hour or so about old times. . . . "Do you remember when?" Then we got around to the current debates about shortcomings in education and the call for a return to basics.

Clara gave me a bemused look. "You know I have to smile every time I hear that word 'basics.' That was all we had at the White House, wasn't it?"

"That's for sure," I said. "The experts today would say we were terribly deprived. What would a health inspector say about us all drinking from one dipper?"

"I guess we shared our diseases." She laughed.

I returned home to find the Tennessee Legislature debating Governor Lamar Alexander's "Master Teacher" program, a plan to recognize and reward outstanding teachers.

I wondered, "What can I give Clara Kent?"

Perhaps this remembrance will do.

SEVEN
The Good Guys Always Won

"Mama, Mama, the Kents have a radio! You can hear people talking from Springfield and Little Rock, and Clara, she [pant, pant] said, we can come and listen tonight. Can we go, Mama? We can hear Lum and Abner, Clara said, and the weatherman from Springfield. Can we go, Mama? Say we will. Please!"

Mama stood there with her mouth open, taking it all in. She had never seen me come running in from school so excited. Not even when Clara had invited us down to hear the first gramophone in the valley. The Kents were always first with any new invention.

"Mama, I'll help you get the little 'uns ready, so we can leave before dark. Please, Mama, please!"

"It's all right with me." Mama chuckled. "I'd like to hear a radio myself. But you have to ask your daddy. He's up at the barn shoeing Ole Babe. And while you're up there, tell him I saw a chicken snake back of the smokehouse."

I flew to the barn, hollering out the news. The startled horse almost kicked Daddy under the chin.

"Aw, I knowed that already," Daddy said. "Howard told me his daddy had ordered one."

"Well, can we go? Please, please, please," I begged.

"I was thinkin' of goin' coon huntin' up around the Throne. Wouldn't you rather help me catch a couple of ringtails?"

Coon hunting, when we could hear a radio for the first time! I started to cry.

"Oh, all right, Son, but you gotta git the chickens fed and the hawgs slopped. You do that and I'll finish this and milk the ole cow."

I moved! I mean, I really moved. When I got back to the house, Mama asked, "Did you tell him about the chicken snake?" I had forgotten.

I had also left the back door open. Brother was out before you could say spit. "Get back in here, Howard Jean," Mama called.

"There he is, Mama!"

Mama stepped out in the yard and that's when she saw the snake go under the house, with Howard crawling after him. "Mercy, mercy, that snake'll bite him! Run and get your daddy while I try to pull your brother out."

Mama snatched Brother from under the floor. Daddy came running and shone his light. He saw the snake and poked it with a hoe handle. Out it came with Brother dancing in glee.

"Kill it, Fred! Kill it!" Mama screamed as she jerked Brother back into the house.

"Whomp! Whomp!" Daddy brought the hoe down on its head and that was the end of Mr. Snake.

When we got to Milton and Nola Kent's, it looked as if the whole valley was there. And people were still coming in with lanterns. I squirmed past the grown-ups and plopped down before the big Philco console beside Cousin Clyde. "This is KWTO, Keep Watching the Ozarks, broadcasting to you from Springfield, Missouri." The deep voice spoke from within the walnut cabinet. I was awestruck.

"Hain't this sumpin!" a bewiskered man chortled from the back of the room. "Here we air at Milton Kent's, way back on Big Creek, and hearin' a feller talk a hundert miles away. If Pa had lived, he never could have b'lieved hit."

"Hesh up, Lige, Ole Man Williford's comin' on."

C.C. Williford was a man destined to become famous in Big Creek Valley. Farmers planted their crops and cut hay by his predictions. Some even came to trust him more than the *Almanac*.

When Ole Man Williford finished his forecast, an announcer asked us to buy Carter's Little Liver Pills, then a friendly fellow said: "Now let's see what's going on down in Pine Ridge." The audience buzzed in anticipation. "Quiet down so's we kin hyar!" Uncle Willie hollered above the hubbub.

"Lum, you remember, wanted to be a piano tuner and sneaked into the Pine Ridge Church one night to practice on the church instrument. Unfortunately he almost ruined it. The pastor had no idea it was Lum and got a bloodhound to sniff out the criminal. Horace the hound picked up Lum's scent and followed him into the Jot 'Em Down Store. As we look in on the old fellers now, Abner is trying to reassure Lum."

ABNER: "Maybe you can outlive him, Lum, he doesn't look too good."

LUM: "If he keeps this up, I won't live too long. Makes me feel guilty havin' a blood hound trailing 'round after me. Uncle Henry Lunceford, he jist thinks the dog likes me."

People were laughing so hard I could hardly hear the dialogue. Uncle Willie was again trying to quiet them down. When they did hush, I knew we had missed something.

Abner was talking to the preacher on the telephone, trying to get the piano out of the church so Lum could have it repaired.

ABNER: "We kin git it fixed for you, Preacher, if only the hammers 'er broke."

LUM: (off mike): "What 'er ye turnin' pale fer, Abner?"

ABNER: "Preacher wants to know how I knows them hammers 'er broke."

LUM: "Now you've done it . . . Horace, lay down there! Horace. . . ."

The music rose above Lum's voice and the announcer came back:

"All right, Lum, let's see if you get out of this pickle. Tune in tomorrow evening folks, same time, same station, and we'll see if Lum gets the pianer fixed or gets in a bigger mess."

A jazz band came on and Milton Kent turned a knob to "off." "Don't reckon nobody wants to hear that stuff," he said. "Better to save the batteries." Clara and her mother-in-law served coffee to the grown-ups and sweet milk to the children. Then everybody started getting their coats and lanterns. "Kin we come back tomorrer night and see if Lum gits the pianer fixed?" someone asked.

"Sure, glad to have ya," Milton said.

But Daddy insisted on going coon hunting and we didn't get back for two nights. By then the store-keepers had the piano out of the church and Grand-papa Spears was checking it out with "Listen to the Mocking Bird." Grandpapa said he had once watched a fellow play this tune on a player piano.

ABNER: "Grandpap, that sounds terrible."

GRANDPA: "Well, that mockin' bird ain't feelin' his level best."

LUM (worried): "This ain't doin' hit at all. Reckon I'll jist hafta pay Cedric Weehunt to haul it to the county seat and have it re-paired."

I never learned if Lum got the piano fixed. Mama felt we were imposing on the Kents by going five nights a week, and Daddy preferred to go coon hunt-ing, anyway. By the time we got back again Lum was in a different jam. He had been tricked into proposing to the Widow Abernathy.

ANNOUNCER: "All Lum's efforts to find a loop-hole to get out of the wedding have failed. It looks like the old boy is doomed for sure this time. As we drop into the Jot 'Em Down Store, Abner is watching the widder coming down the street to see her in-tended."

ABNER: "Law, will ye look at that pigeon-toed hat she's wearin'. Some rooster over at her place must be freezin' to death."

LUM: "Looks lak a dadburned Indian, if ye want my opinion. Looks lak she's all set for a Choctaw war dance."

ABNER: "Lum, git yer hands down off yer eyes. She's a comin' in here to see ye."

LUM: "Abner, there's a limit at what a man kin stand to see."

Lum must have escaped, for the next week he was in another mess and nothing was said about him being married.

After Daddy started working for the WPA, he got home too late for us to go week nights. Saturday night was the Grand Ole Opry "comin' to you from clear channel Double W S M in Nashville, Tennessee. Let 'er go, boys!" Daddy and the men stomped the floor, keeping time with the Gully Jumpers, the Fruit-jar Drinkers, the 'Possum Hunters, and Uncle Dave Macon. I waited patiently for my favorites, Jamup and Honey, and though it might be late (the Opry lasted four hours), I never felt unrewarded.

HONEY: "Jamup, I'se hears somethin' on the porch."

JAMUP (sleepily): "See whut it is, and let me git some shuteye. May jist be yer old hound dawg."

HONEY: "I think hit's in this room. Hit hain't my dawg. . . . Hand me that ole twelve-gauge."

JAMUP (still asleep): "Git it y'erself."

HONEY: "Hit's comin' closer. Hit's. . . . Stay where ye air, ye no good varmint! Don't move, 'er I'll shoot! I'm a warnin' ye!"

Boom!

HONEY: "Yeooooooow, oo, oh, me, I'm a dyin'. Light that lamp, Jamup. Ohhhh, ohhhhh."

JAMUP (awake): "I got the light on. Now let's see. . . . Oh, there's blood all ober de foot of de bed. Ye've kilt somethin' shore."

HONEY: "Ohhhhhh, ohhhhhh. . . . I think I've kilt myself."

JAMUP: "Naw, ye ain't. I kin see now. Ye've jist shot off y'er big toe. . . ."

One Tuesday Glenn and Emma came to school, big grins wrapped around their faces. "Pa got us a radio," Glenn crowed. "Last evenin' we heerd Tom Mix and Jack Armstrong!"

"And The Lone Ranger and The Squeakin' Door!" Emma added.

"Inner Sanctum," Glenn corrected. "Come on onct a week. Scarier stuff than Pa kin tell. Jack Armstrong and the Ranger comes on fifteen minutes every evenin', Monday through Friday. And Tom Mix too. He comes on last."

I waited until supper to spring this news on Mama and Daddy. Then: "If Uncle Willie can git a radio, why can't we?"

"We can't afford it," Mama said sadly. "It would take as much as your daddy makes in a month."

I kept asking . . . and asking. No kid ever wanted anything worse in his life. Glenn and Emma telling me about what happened the evening before only made the longing worse. Oh, how I pleaded!

Finally—the next summer—Mama filled out an order blank in the Sears & Roebuck catalog and gave that and a wad of one-dollar bills she had been saving to Uncle Elmer, the mail carrier. "Get us a money order at the Judy post office and send off for our radio," she said. Uncle Elmer really was my uncle.

He was married to my Aunt Viola, Daddy's oldest sister.

The next day I saw Uncle Elmer riding up the creek road with the mail bags. "Didja send off our order?" I asked.

"Shore did."

"When will it come?"

"When hit gits hyar."

The new school term began. Uncle Elmer usually passed by a little after the morning recess. I kept my eye fastened on the window and when I saw him coming with a package tied to his saddle horn, I asked to go to the outhouse. I ran and stopped the mail carrier instead.

"No, this ain't yer radio," he said. The next day Uncle Elmer went hunting and Aunt Viola rode by with the mail: "No, this package is fer Bryants."

The next, Uncle Elmer: "Yep, I've got somethin' for ye. Mou't jist be yer radio."

I thought Clara would never ring the closing bell. When she did I took off like a scalded dog. I cut across the Reddell's pasture without even looking to see if the billy goat was close by. I raced past the mulberry tree, splashed across the creek, ran through Grandpa Tom's cotton patch, past his house, and up the hill.

"Mama, where's the radio? Uncle Elmer said he had it," I panted.

Then I saw the box in the corner with SILVER-TONE RADIO stenciled across the top. "Whoopeeee! Take it out, Mama, and make it play!"

"It's stayin' in that box 'til your daddy gets home. He has to put up an aerial before you can hear."

"Why can't you, Mama?"

"I can't climb on top of the house. Now, go play with your brother and the twins, while I work on supper. And try not to wake Jimmie Fern up. Your daddy will be here in a little while."

That little while stretched like an eternity. At last he clomped through the door, saw the box, and grinned. He took out the shiny walnut cabinet and the dry cell battery which was heavier than the radio. He put both on the shelf under the window sill and ran the aerial wire under the window. We went outside and made a ground, then he climbed to the roof and strung the other wire across the top of the house.

"Turn it on!" I squealed, when we were back inside.

He twisted a knob. Click. Just a few crackles of static. He twirled the other knob and I saw the red frequency needle move across to the far left of the dial and stop on fifty-five.

". . . Tom and his pals are hanging from trees. The rawhide around their neck is stretching tighter and tighter. The pain is crawling down their arms, into their chests, down their legs. Can they escape? Tune in tomorrow for the surprising climax and hear another episode of Tom Mix, America's favorite cowboy."

"Up, Tony, come on, boy!" I heard Tom say. Then he sang,

> *Hot Ralston for your breakfast*
> *Starts the day off shining bright.*
> *Gives you lots of cowboy energy*
> *With a flavor that's just right.*

It's delicious and nutritious;
Made of golden Western wheat;
So take a tip from Tom.
Go and tell your Mom,
'Hot Ralston can't be beat.'

Tom Mix was off the air. I had missed all the serials that evening.

But we heard Ole Man Williford, Lum and Abner, and a sticky story from Hollywood called, Lux Radio Theater. I would have stayed up all night, but Mama insisted that I blow out the lamp and come to bed.

Just as Ole Man Williford predicted, a storm swept in the next afternoon. You think I'd take shelter at a house or under a bluff with that radio at home? I ran all the way and got soaked.

Ignoring Mama's plea to "get some dry clothes on before you catch a cold," I turned on the radio. "Crackle, pop. Pop, pop, pop, crackle." It was set on KWTO. I turned the volume up. "CRACKLE, POP, POP, POP, CRACKLE."

I jammed my ear against the speaker and heard ever so faintly, "Jack Armstrong, Jack Armstrong. . . ." Then the sound faded and only the static was there.

"Might as well turn it off," Mama said sadly. "No reason to run the battery down when you can't hear."

What a dreary afternoon that turned out to be! Reception after dark was no better and I went to bed cramped with disappointment.

Whooooeeee! The sky was clear as a robin's egg the next day.

When I got home I turned on the Silvertone and heard some blood-stirring music, then,

"With his faithful Indian companion, Tonto, the daring and resourceful Masked Rider of the Plains led the fight for law and order in the early western United States. Nowhere in the pages of history can one find a greater champion of justice! Return with us now to those thrilling days of yesteryear! From out of the past come the thundering hoofbeats of the great horse, Silver! The Lone Ranger rides again!"

"Come on, Silver!"

"Git 'um up, Scout!"

"Hi, yo, Silver, awa-a-a-a-ay!"

I didn't breathe until the station break and commercial.

Then, joy, oh joy, came the steamboat cheer for what would become my favorite:

"Jack Armstrong. . . . Jack Armstrong. . . . JACK ARMSTRONG. . . . *JACK ARMSTRONG*, THE ALL-AMERICAN BOY. . . ."

> *Wave the flag for Hudson High, boys,*
> *Show them how we stand!*
> *Ever shall our team be champions*
> *Known throughout the land.*

The announcer gave a spiel for Wheaties, then Jack and his buddy, Billy Fairfield, and Billy's sister, Betty, were off on another "thrill-packed" adventure.

After Jack Armstrong, Tom Mix, owner of the TM Bar Ranch, came galloping out of the airways. While Tom and his Straight-Shooter pals were battling a bunch of "low-down, side-winders," Daddy arrived back from milking eager to hear Ole Man Williford.

When the weather man signed off, Mama insisted—ordered—us both to supper.

I tried vainly to get attention, anybody's attention. Daddy was wolfing his food down. The twins and Jimmie Fern were crying. "Fred, help me get something down these young'uns' throats." Brother was dropping bread crumbs under the table to Ole Lion who had snuck in behind Daddy returning from the barn. "Fred, put that old dog out. Howard Jean, tend to your own business and eat."

Didn't they want to hear how the Lone Ranger had rescued the rancher's golden-haired daughter from the black-hearted villain? Didn't they care that Jack and Billy and Betty had discovered a "lost world" deep inside the earth? And that Tom Mix and his Straight Shooters were surrounded by an army of mean cattle rustlers when Tom's program went off the air?

Howard Jean: "Mama, Louise spit in my milk."

Mama: "Fred, now you let Ole Muse in when you were puttin' Ole Lion out."

Daddy: "Heah, heah, Muse. Git out, dawg. I'll feed ye in a minute."

They didn't care.

After supper, I helped Daddy in the barn. Then we came back to the house for more listening.

"Weowwwwwwwwwww! Weowwwwwwwwwww! Weowwwwwwwwwww! Ack-ack-ack-ack-ack-ack. Clomp! Clomp! Clomp!" The sirens, the rattle of machine guns, the sound of prisoners' marching feet heralded GANGBUSTERS!

Crooks break into a store: "Slam! Smash! Crash! Tinkle, tinkle, tinkle! Thump-thump-thump."

An inner door opens: "Click."

The frightened merchant asks fearfully: "What, who are you?"

The chief felon snarls: "Show us where the safe is, Buster, or we'll plug your gizzard."

"No, no!" The old man refuses.

"Sock! Pop! Wham!" They beat him until he tells.

"Bang, bang. Orrrrrrggghhhh. Ahhhhhhh. Thud." The old man falls to the floor—dead.

Then: "Police! Hold it! We've got ya cornered. Come out with your hands up. Don't try anything funny."

One crook makes a break. "Bang, bang, bang. Yeowwwwwwww, ya winged me in the shoulder, copper. Don't shoot! We're comin' out."

The murdering thugs are captured. Off to jail they go.

How much excitement can a boy take? But wait, there's more for this evening.

"Squeeeeeeeeeeeeeeeakkkk. Ka-THUNK!"

"Good evening, friends. This is Raymond, your host, welcoming you in through the squeaking door to the 'Inner Sanctum.' We have another tale to thrill you, and to chill you. Please come in and have a seat. Oh, you don't believe in vampires and zombies and ghosts. Well, our tale tonight is about a man who didn't believe in them either. He found out he was wrong . . . dead wrong. Ha-ha-ha-ha-haaaa."

"Bromoseltzerbromoseltzerbromoseltzer. . . ."
Faster and faster chugs the talking train, then comes the bloodcurdling story of the nice old doctor with a hypodermic needle who turns out to be a vampire.

Night after night, I sat glued beside that radio. Until the battery power faded. Then we had to wait until Daddy sold his furs, then till Uncle Elmer delivered the mail-order package on his horse. I never learned how Jack Armstrong and his pals escaped from being thrown in the lake of fire in the center of the earth. Or how the Masked Rider of the Plains and faithful Tonto fought their way out of a box canyon, against the blazing guns of thirty cold-eyed outlaws.

But when the battery came, such disappointments were forgotten. The radio had power and all was right in my world.

The romances and the silly comedies could pass. Give me the afternoon adventure serials and the evening crime shows and mysteries.

The Green Hornet (alias Brit Reid, young publisher of the *Daily Sentinel*) was a citified version of the Lone Ranger. Both wore a mask. The Ranger had his great white stallion; the Hornet his superpowered Black Beauty car, equipped with a buzzing Hornet horn. The Ranger loaded his six-guns with silver bullets; the Hornet carried a pistol primed with puffs of deadly gas. The Ranger had his faithful Tonto; the Hornet his loyal Kato.

Of all the mysteries, I liked "I love a Mystery" best. A train whistle shrieked through the night and the three swashbucklers of mystery—Jack, Doc, and Reggie—were on the air.

I traveled with Jack, Doc, and Reggie to the Temple of the Jaguar in a cave on the Island of the Skulls. Jack and Doc were trying to rescue two kidnapped girls about to be sacrificed by the cruel high priest, Holy Joe. While Jack climbs a spiderweb of ropes to rescue the girls from a bamboo cage, Doc confronts the villain on the upper catwalk a hundred feet above the temple floor. "The first move you make in this direction, you're a dead pigeon," Doc warns. Holy Joe doesn't believe the smiling Texan has a gun in his pocket and moves on him. A shot echoes through the gigantic cavern. "Aaagh! Aaagh!" Holy Joe falls to his death.

"I got him, Jack," Doc calls. "Honest to my grandma."

Doc was my favorite of the three. I sealed every promise with that line.

"Mama, I'm going to get Brother out of the chicken coop. Honest to my grandma."

"Yes, Daddy, I've finished slopping the hogs. Honest to my grandma."

"I saw two 'possums on the way to school this morning. Honest to my grandma."

In those tranquil days of sweet simplicity, you could easily separate the good guys from the villains. Honest to my grandma. The good guys, like Sergeant Preston of the Yukon, "led the fight for law and order." They always won. The G-Men got Dillinger. Tom Mix whipped the treacherous renegade, Bear Claw. The Masked Rider of the Plains put the notorious Butch Cavendish behind bars. Truth and virtue always reaped a reward, evil never went unpunished.

Some of the night fighters were not quite paragons of virtue. But the serial heroes could do no wrong. Brave, dauntless, and true was Jack Armstrong. Would Jack lie? Did an eagle have horns like a billy goat? Jack was the kind who would grow up to be president of the United States.

They were proud to be Americans. "Train to be an American," Jack's announcer challenged. "Follow Jack Armstrong's rules for physical fitness: Get plenty of fresh air, sleep, and exercise. Use lots of soap and water every day. Eat the kind of breakfast America needs in times like these—milk, fruit, and Wheaties—breakfast of champions!"

I didn't have Wheaties. It hurt not to have boxtops to send for the Magic Cat's Eye Ring that glowed like a tiger's eye. I didn't use lots of soap and water. Have you ever seen what lye soap does to hands? But I got plenty of fresh air, sleep, and exercise, along with heaping helpings of heroics from my idols.

Ah, those sweet memories of radio yore! Whenever I hear Rossini's *William Tell Overture*, I still want to shout, "Hi, yo, Silver, awa-a-a-a-ay!"—if nobody's around.

Maybe the characters were too good to be true. Maybe they should have messed up once in awhile. Maybe they should have hinted that some families break up and some men and women have sex outside marriage. Maybe they did lack realism.

We've got "realism" now in electronic entertainment, they say.

Really?

Times have changed, the media moguls say. We're just reflecting society in which seven hundred thousand children were born last year out of wedlock and over a million marriages dissolved.

The media merchants are reflecting morals, all right—their own morals.

And the media has no impact, they say.

Horsefeathers! If the media don't influence people strongly, why do we have commercials?

Granted, we can't turn back completely to the days when right was always right and wrong always wrong, and good guys always won. When we were sold patriotism, respect for parents, and love of truth and country. When bad guys were not dressed up good and good guys not painted bad.

It would be unreal to go completely back.

But if there's a choice, I'll take Jack Armstrong and Tom Mix anytime over Dallas and General Hospital.

It's a matter of decency and values.

Honest to my grandma.

EIGHT
Moving Up

Our home was five miles and five creek fords from Mt. Judy when I finished the eighth grade at the White House. The creek was often out of its banks for a week or more at a time. The only other way to Judy then was around the mountain benches, through deep woods, and along the top of several high bluffs. Too risky for a nine-year-old boy going by himself. Even when the creek was low, the trip to high school would take four hours, round trip.

There was never any question about whether I would go. "James Carl is going to get educated and make something of himself," Mama declared. "And the rest of our children will come right behind him."

The only way was to move.

Daddy sold our sixty-one acres to the Ozark National Forest for $244. The Forest had no use for the old house and barn, so Uncle Vester hauled away the logs.

Daddy bought a little forty-acre farm a mile north of Judy on State Route 123. It came with an unpainted four-room frame house, cistern, barn, and pond. All for $250. And we also got electricity soon after moving in.

We moved after the winter term closed at the White House, in time for Mama to plant a garden and for Daddy and me to clear some new ground and plant a corn crop. Daddy bought a couple of cows and planned to raise hay on the land that had been cleared before he bought the place.

You'd think Mama would be satisfied with raising kids and putting in a garden. You didn't know Mama. Now that we had electricity, she bought a cream separator and started selling milk. Then she said, "Fred, build us a chicken house. We're going to sell eggs too."

Grandpa Pulliam, Mama's daddy, came from way over on Honey Creek. He and Daddy put up that chicken house, about ten by fifteen feet, in less than three weeks. Mama came out as they were finishing up the frame and noted it had just one flaw. "Where's the door?" She laughed. Daddy stood back and looked. Then he grinned at Grandpa. "I'll be dawged, Pulliam—we fergot to make a place for Hester to go in and git the aigs."

You'd think that would be enough for Mama. No, indeed, she had to start a store in one of the front rooms. "We got by living in two rooms up the creek," she said. "We'll have three rooms here and still have a place for a store."

It wasn't quite a store at first. What she did was walk out to Judy and bargain with Cousin Lloyd, who ran the biggest store in Judy. "I'll buy six boxes of nickel baking soda, if you'll sell them to me for a quarter," she offered. That way she could make a nickel profit. Buying small quantities like that and putting her profits back into the business, she was able to stock the store room with necessities. Close neighbors would come over and buy a small item from Mama and save the long walk into Judy. She also sold to visiting kinfolks. "Look in the store and see if there's anything you need." And, "Wouldn't you rather give me your business than to trade at Judy?" Mama may have had the first "convenience" store in the county, even the state.

By the time the corn was laid by in late June, I was eager for a rest. School wouldn't start at Judy until August. I would be there for eight months, since Judy didn't have a split term like the one-room schools.

"Not yet," Daddy said. "I need you to help haul the rocks out of the hay field. So I can cut the oats with a sickle," he explained.

I thought I would die under that Ozark sun picking up rocks and throwing them in the sled. If there had been a market for limestone and flint rocks, Newton County would have been the richest county in America.

When the rocks were hauled there was time for play. Luckily, Mama's sister, Aunt Ethel Freeman, and her family put up a tent just a few hundred yards down the road. The oldest boy, a redhead named Paul, was just a year older than me. His brother Junior was close to Howard Jean.

Paul and I considered Howard and Junior mean little rascals. They tried to live up to that reputation. One morning they stomped every melon in Daddy's watermelon patch. We older brothers watched in glee as Daddy and Uncle Ernie gave them stinging doses of corrective medicine.

A few days later Paul and I met at a big pine to go robin hunting. We came armed with new beanflips (slingshots) and pockets full of pebbles. Howard sneaked up from behind and grabbed my weapon, while Junior snatched Paul's.

"We'll git you fer that," Paul hollered, as they ran cackling into a thicket.

"Where air you hiding?" we demanded, parting briars right and left. "We're goin' ta find ye."

A screech came from above. Then: "Yah, yah, you'uns ain't goin' robin huntin' today." There they were, perched on a limb of a small red oak about fifteen feet above the ground, dangling our beanflips provocatively.

"Throw 'em down," Paul yelled.

"Come and git us," Junior taunted back.

Paul started up the tree and the two little monkeys climbed higher. He saw that if he went much further the little tree would break. He leaped to the ground.

We looked at our brothers in the tree, then at each other. We were thinking the same thing.

"Go git yer daddy's choppin' ax. I'll keep 'em up thar," Paul said.

I ran for the ax.

"Throw down air beanflips, or we'll chop the tree down with ye," Paul threatened.

"Try'n make us," Junior taunted.

Paul swung and the chips began to fly. Then I took a turn. I kept thinking that surely they would come down.

Crack! Paul and I jumped back. The tree split where we had been chopping. Our brothers rode it down part way, then jumped, landing with thuds.

I grabbed our weapons. Paul helped them up. "Ye all right?"

Junior glared at him and took off running with Howard panting behind him. My brother admitted later that it was the hardest fall he ever took.

Daddy was working in the field and Mama had her egg, milk, and store business to tend to, besides three little girls. Howard and I did about what we wanted the rest of the summer. One day we walked a mile to the creek and caught a string of perch. The next we went rabbit hunting. Mama and Daddy never knew where we were until we came back in the evening.

Once I was out by myself, digging a rabbit out of a rock pile. I just happened to look over, and there, a foot from my left hand, reared a big ole copperhead, poisonous as a rattlesnake, darting his tongue at me. I leaped back just in time, scrambled to my feet, and ran for a hoe. When I got back, he was gone.

Another morning Daddy was in the field and Mama had gone into Judy. Howard and I were supposed to be watching the girls. We found a couple of old tires that had been dumped by a road and started rolling them downhill with the twins and Jimmie Fern following.

The tires rolled off into a little hollow. "Come on," I yelled back at my brother and sisters. Mine wobbled over a huge nest of yellow jackets. The angry insects rose in a fog. "Run!" I screamed.

Howard and the twins took off hollering, yellow jackets stinging them on the head, neck, arms, and legs. Little Jimmie Fern, paralyzed with fear, plopped smack down in the nest, shrieking in terror. I grabbed her up and raced after the others.

Mama almost went hysterical when she saw the girls. "Mercy, mercy! What did you get them into, James Carl? It's a wonder they weren't stung to death."

Jimmie still has the scars to show for it.

A few days before school was to start, Howard and I were sent to gather a sack of walnuts for drying in the barn. If we had done what we were told and no more, there would have been no problem.

We decided to sample a few and began peeling off the pulpy hulls to get at the inner nut. We came home with hands, arms, and feet stained green.

Mama went at us with lye soap. "Didn't you think about how hard walnut stain would be to get off?" she reminded.

"Yes, Mama. Uh, ouch! That hurts. Mama, you're takin' skin and all. Mama, I need to go to the outhouse. Ouch, Mama, ouch!"

When she got through we looked like we had leprosy, and she still hadn't gotten all the stain off. We had to go to school looking like that.

Leaving the girls with Daddy, Mama walked Howard and me to our first day of school. She took Brother to the second grade teacher in the smaller frame building that sat beside the larger stone structure, housing the seventh and eighth grades and the high school.

Mama then took me to the superintendent in the tiny ten-by-ten-foot library off in a corner from the big high school home room. She introduced me and said, "Clara Kent says he's ready for the ninth grade."

The school official eyed me with suspicion. A skinny, gawky little black-haired kid, wearing a new shirt and overalls, but barefooted and hands spotted with walnut stains. "He's a little stunted in growth, isn't he, Hester?"

"Oh, he's the right size for his age. He just turned nine, the second of last June."

"You foolin' me, Hester?"

"No, Sir. He could read when he was three. Clara Kent let him take two grades a year."

I could tell the superintendent was still doubtful. "We, uh, have never taken a nine-year-old into high school before. I, uh, will have to talk with my principal. Oh, there he is now. Joe, come over here a minute and look at this boy. Hester says he's ready for the ninth grade."

The principal just stared at me. Finally he said, "He don't look no bigger than a third grader to me."

"Hester," the superintendent said, "take your boy outside for a minute while we decide what to do with him."

I felt like a monkey on display.

After a few minutes, the superintendent came out to see us. "Hester, we've decided to enter him in the eighth and see how he does."

Mama's patience was about exhausted. "He's already had the eighth I told you. He finished up six months ago."

"Hester, he's too little for high school. The big kids will tromp all over him. Take him to Herbert Edwards in the eighth grade room."

Herbert was a near neighbor. He was writing an assignment on the blackboard when we entered and Mama beckoned him over. I felt at ease with Herbert. He and I had had a few conversations about the war in Europe. "Well, James Carl," he said grinning, "do you think Hitler is going to invade Poland?"

"If he does," I said, "England and France will declare war on him."

"You think so?"

"That's what Gabriel Heatter said last night on the radio."

Herbert turned to Mama. "What's the problem, Hester? I thought he was ready for high school."

"He *is*," Mama said firmly. "They say he's too little and that he must take the eighth grade over."

"We'll be glad to have him." Herbert smiled.

"I don't reckon they'll change their minds?" Mama asked.

Herbert shook his head. "They're the law here."

"I guess he's yours. I'm sorry about the walnut stain. I scrubbed and scrubbed. I just couldn't get it all off."

Herbert knew little boys. "It'll wear off in time. Go on home, Hester, I'll take good care of him."

He marched me to the front of the room and faced the students. "Boys and girls, meet the youngest member of our class, my new neighbor, James Carl

Hefley. We're going to see what he can do."

Herbert threw down a challenge and I ate it up. I led the class. Herbert was amazed at my math skills and said he had never had a boy so smart. I loved that and only felt determined to try harder.

Howard Jean, sad to say, was a colt of a different color. He would not stay in school. Mama would walk him all the way and the minute she'd leave, he'd scat out the first open window.

"I don't see why you can't be like your big brother," Mama said when she got a truancy report from the teacher. "He loves school. Don't you, James Carl?"

I nodded, then handed my brother a smirk. That's the way it went for the rest of the school year, me making As and Howard playing hooky.

When school was out the following March, I brought home a stack of books from the little library. "I hope you left a few," Mama said proudly.

I plunged into Osa Johnson's *I Married Adventure* and was transported to Africa, facing ferocious lions and dodging headhunters, when Daddy snapped me out of my reverie. "Corn plantin' time," he said. To my dismay, he had rented an extra ten acres from his Uncle Bill (Grandpa Tom's brother). It was so far from the house that we had to take our dinner. I wanted to take my book, but he said, "No, we've got work to do." The next few days seemed to drag on forever. Then and there I vowed that when I grew up I would not be a farmer. The days were too long, the work too hard.

I had never had any money of my own. Sometimes when we were in Judy, if I begged long enough,

Mama would buy me a nickel bottle of pop. When I asked for a nickel or dime, she usually said, "You'd just waste it."

One day she sat me down in the store room to explain the economic facts of life. "Nothing comes free," she said.

"There are only four ways to make money," she continued. "You can persuade somebody to give you some, and that isn't likely—not from me. You can steal and that isn't right. You can work and produce something somebody else wants and will pay you money for. Or you can buy something and resell it and make a profit."

"I'll buy and sell for a profit," I said.

"What do you have to buy it with?" she teased.

"Aw, Mama, you know I don't have any money."

"All right, then think, what can you produce to sell?"

Instantly: "I know, Mama. I'll dig some roots. Will you go and help me find the right kind?"

She wisely shook her head. "You'll have to find your own. I can't leave the little girls."

I felt stupid for not thinking of this sooner. With the war in Europe and Asia, slippery elm and black haw bark, mayapple, and ginseng were all in demand for making medicines. The difficulty was that every-thing was dug up within a few miles around Judy. I got a hoe and went to look anyway.

I found a little black haw tree that had been missed about a half mile from our house. It was on Preacher Ester Holt's land, but I didn't think of that. A product that I could sell was there for the digging. I dug down deep and pried up the long, tapering roots. Then I peeled off the bark with my Barlow knife and stuffed the precious substance in a paper poke.

Judy, here I come. Charlie Jones' store was on Highway 123 just before the road made a sharp left turn up the dirt road that ran through Judy. I ran into Charlie's in a fever and thrust my precious poke on the counter. "I have some black haw root bark to sell," I said grandly.

Charlie poured the bark onto his scale, squinting at the figures beside the quivering red needle while I held my breath. "Hmmm, it stops on fifty-three cents. You made a big dig, Son."

I was rich! And nobody but Charlie and I knew.

"Cash or trade?"

My eyes were roving across the glass candy counter. "Trade! I'll take two Paydays, a Milky Way, a Snickers, and a Three Musketeers."

"Whoa, I can't keep count. You sure you want it all in candy?"

I nodded greedily.

I picked out nine nickel chocolate and peanut bars, a nickel's worth of Kits' caramels, and three penny suckers. I ran out of the store, clutching the poke to my chest and grinning.

I ate every piece on the way home, even to polishing off the suckers. I had begun to feel uncomfortable after the fifth bar, and now cramps were coming on.

Mama immediately noticed the chocolate around my mouth. "Where have you been, James Carl? What have you been into?"

I didn't say a word.

"Where have you been, Son? What have you been into?" she repeated.

"To the store. To sell my bark. Mama, I'm sick. Mama, I'm dyin'. Ohhhhhhh, Mama, Mama, help me. Urp, urp, urp." I threw up on the floor.

Howard was snickering, the twins giggling. Mama laid me down and draped a cold washcloth over my forehead, then cleaned up the floor.

"You feelin' better?" Mama asked.

I managed a weak smile.

"How much did you get for your bark?"

"Fifty-three cents."

"You took it all in candy?"

"Uh, huh."

"You ate all the candy? You didn't think of your brother and sisters?"

"Uhh, huh . . . I ate the whole poke full."

"I can't believe it. You blew fifty-three cents on candy? And all for yourself?" I could see the wheels turning in her head.

I rubbed my sore belly. "I'm sorry, Mama. I'll never do it again. Honest to my grandma."

She managed a smile. "Well, I reckon you have learned a lesson. I should have told you about saving money and sharing."

"I didn't think of that."

"Well, next time, do."

That wasn't my best summer. The cistern went dry, then the spring down the hill where we got drinking water stopped running. We had to walk and carry water from a spring at the creek, a mile away. I also got hit by a stinging lizard while lifting up a rock. It was like being stung by ten wasps at once. My hand ached for two days.

It didn't help that our Freeman relatives folded up their tent and moved to a house several miles away. I still saw Paul and Junior occasionally, but it wasn't like living within hollering distance.

Uncle Ernie Freeman had a reputation of being a moonshiner and a tough guy. He knew all the outlaws, and if there was any trouble about to happen on Big Creek he usually knew about it in advance.

The most notorious outlaw was a man I'll call Ole Caterwaul. He heard about Newton County while serving in the Arkansas State Penitentiary. A county native, serving time then, told him, "I know a place where's you kin hide out ferever." When his sentence was up, Ole Caterwaul headed for our neck of the woods.

You could find people who would defend Ole Caterwaul. Grandpa Pulliam let him stay in his barn on Honey Creek. "He ain't never done me no harm," Grandpa said. "There ain't no way he could do everything they accuse him of."

It's true that too much meanness was laid on Ole Caterwaul. His defenders also swore that he only robbed well-off people—which usually meant stores—and gave to the poor.

Uncle Ernie heard by the grapevine that Ole Caterwaul was going to try to rob us and warned Daddy to be prepared. Daddy began leaving his double-barreled twenty-gauge shotgun, loaded with buckshot, beside his bed in the front room.

A few days later, Daddy heard the door latch rattle. "Who's there?" he called.

The intruder did not answer and kept finagling the door latch.

"Answer er I'll shoot," Daddy demanded.

Still no identification. Daddy aimed low and pulled the trigger. Then he ran and pushed the door open and shot again at the shadowy figure dashing across the yard.

Howard Jean and I, occupying a bed in the next room, slept through it all. But the next morning the hole in the front door was plain to see. "Ole Caterwaul tried to get in," Daddy explained. "I hope I skeered him off."

Uncle Ernie heard about the attempted robbery and came over the next afternoon, bringing his pistol. "He'll be back tonight," he predicted. "He don't give up."

The sun was down and shadows were creeping across the hayfield. Daddy was down at the barn milking and Uncle Ernie was standing guard with his pistol. Howard and I were listening to Jack Armstrong and watching out the window. When the program went off I stepped out into the yard. Mama was busy in the kitchen.

I heard Uncle Ernie yell, "Thar he is! Hold it! Hold it, or I'll shoot ye!" I reckon Ole Caterwaul didn't hold it, for Uncle Ernie began blazing away. He and Daddy raced through the field after him, but Old Caterwaul outran them both. Next morning they tracked him across two hollows and found the ashes still warm where he had camped in the corn patch we had planted on Uncle Bill's land.

Ole Caterwaul never bothered us again. Daddy later joined a posse to hunt him down. They were in the woods when Daddy saw a man coming whom he thought was Ole Caterwaul. He lifted his shotgun and was about to pull the trigger when the fellow saw him and yelled. He was a deputy sheriff. Years after this a U.S. Marshal tricked the outlaw into surrendering with the promise of a job as a forest ranger. They put him in jail, but he escaped and never came back to Newton County.

Not long after Ole Caterwaul tried to rob us a man wearing a necktie drove up in a shiny new car. He and Mama and Daddy talked, then Daddy signed some papers and passed him five ten dollar bills.

"Who was he?" I asked Mama eagerly.

"That's Roy Milum, the state senator," she said. Then I remembered seeing his name on the vacant store where Highway 123 turned up the main street of Judy.

"We're going into the store business big," Mama announced with a broad smile. "What do you think of that?"

I liked the idea. Being in a store, having all the candy and pop I wanted to eat. "We're moving to Judy, Mama?"

"No, we'll stay here for right now. Your daddy will keep on farming."

What a letdown.

They signed to pay five hundred dollars for the eighty-by-thirty-foot frame building, including all the shelving and counters. The terms were fifty dollars down and ten dollars a month.

Daddy moved the groceries from the store room to the store in Judy. Then they bought ten dollars more stock from the wholesale salesman to be delivered by the truck the next day. When the salesman came back the next week they used the profit to add to their order.

Except for Jones' Grocery on the west all the businesses in Judy were on the north side of the road. Our store was on the corner in front of Jones' store, then Doc Sexton and Doc Blackwood's little office, then Cousin Lloyd's store and post office. Cousin Gussie and her husband, Jeames Nichols, had the cafe, just beyond Lloyd's store. A wag described Judy in rhyme.

> *Jones' Store and Hefley's street*
> *Nichols' Cafe and Nuthin' to eat.*

That wasn't quite true. You could get a good baloney sandwich from Cousin Gussie, and if you waited a while she would fry you a hamburger.

And there was more to the town. Down the hill, John Johnson operated the big steam-powered mill that ginned cotton, sawed lumber, and ground corn. Wes Berry had the hotel, across the street from Lloyd's store. The hotel was really just an overgrown two-story bungalow with a balcony running across the front of the second floor.

Our store looked so big it seemed you could almost get lost in it. It had big plate glass windows in front with window wells behind where hangers-on could sit. A large potbellied stove squatted in the center with an old washpan at the mouth for a spittoon. Shelves and glass-topped counters ran up and down the sides and there was a feed room in back. Our first order of groceries didn't fill up a single shelf.

Six days a week, Mama got up and cooked breakfast, made the beds, then headed down the road to Judy, carrying her sixth child, Freddie Gelese—a name Mama made up—and leading Jimmie Fern. The twins toddled behind and Howard Jean brought up the rear, looking for an opportunity to dart off the road and keep from going to school. Sometimes I helped her with Jimmie Fern. Other times I ran ahead and was waiting on the store porch for the rest to arrive. Most mornings, Daddy stayed behind to do farm chores, coming later in the day to help Mama in the store.

This became too much. They sold the farm on Route 123 and bought a house in Judy. We moved around the town four times, finally ending up living behind a partition built by Daddy across the back of the store. Mama was always being called out of the house at night to get groceries for someone. "We might as well move into the store," she told Daddy.

Daddy was not lazy. He just refused to be caged up in the store twenty-four hours a day. He bought a Model T pickup and ran a grocery route around the south end of the county. He traded store goods for fur and roots and an occasional hound pup.

Mama was not happy about the dogs. "Fred, you've already got six hounds. How can we afford to feed another?"

"Aw, I'm gonna train 'em to tree coons and sell 'em to rich fellers up north."

It wasn't long until he had eleven hounds baying and yelping in a fenced lot we owned across the road. Mama said the dogs would eat us into the poorhouse, and that he loved his dogs more than her.

Without telling Mama, he put an ad in a coon hunter's magazine. One afternoon he came from the post office grinning like a ground squirrel. He held up a fifty-dollar money order before Mama's eyes. "That's just the deposit for Ole Blue. I'm shipping him C.O.D. from Harrison. A feller in Ohio is to pay me $350 more on delivery. I only paid twenty-five dollars for him when he was a pup," he added gleefully.

Mama looked that money order over to see if it was genuine. She read the letter twice to see if it was really true.

Daddy was still grinning all over. "An', I've got two more over thar that will bring three or four hundert dollars apiece by summer."

Mama didn't complain nearly so much after that.

Mama found her niche in that store. She and Daddy would be in the general merchandise business for the next thirty-eight years. Daddy worked about half time in the store, helping Mama, cutting hair for twenty-five cents a head with never a day of barber training. His big interest remained with training coon hounds. He traveled thousands of miles, entering his dogs in coon dog field trials, winning money and a roomful of trophies. He became without doubt the champion coon hunter of Newton County.

Mama's one business weakness was that she couldn't turn away anybody who wanted credit. Some would run up a big bill with her. Then, after getting paid for a cache of furs or a load of lumber, they'd go up and pay cash with Cousin Lloyd or Charlie Jones. Mama would see them go in and come out of a competitor's store with a big bag of groceries and shake her head sorrowfully. We'd say, "Mama, send them a bill and demand payment."

"No," she'd answer. "They know that they owe us and it will be on their conscience."

I reckon a good many had weak consciences. After Mama was put in the nursing home, I found a box full of old bills in a closet. Some of the deadbeats were among the most prominent people in Big Creek Valley. I'm not naming them here. But they know. They know.

Mama and Daddy were entrepreneurs in different ways. Mama was the mainstay, but she was a slave to work. Daddy enjoyed what he did. I reckon he took his hunting after Grandpa Tom and his trading after Grandpa Jim. Cousin Glenn told me recently, "Your daddy is the only man I ever knew who could make money off of ole hound dogs."

Glenn and I talked about Mama as a merchant. "She lived in a place and time when married women were expected to do little but keep house and raise kids," I noted. "Where did she get her business drive?"

"Your mama was a born merchant," he said.

"I know that. But that doesn't explain her grit and determination."

"Don't you see?" Glenn declared. "It was her kids—you and the rest. She wanted her children to have a better chance at life than she had."

NINE
Monk and 'Fesser

My first day of high school. I bounced in barefooted, eager to get going. "Where do the ninth graders sit?" I asked C. B. Hudson.

He waved his hand. "On the left side next to the windows."

Freshmen, sophomores, juniors, and seniors were all in the same big room. As you advanced in status, you merely moved a few rows to the right. You also got cooler in winter time, since the cast-iron wood stove was in the freshmen's section.

There was a stage in front of the big room with a canvas curtain that proclaimed MOUNT JUDEA HIGH SCHOOL and asked you to shop at LLOYD HEFLEY'S GENERAL MERCHANDISE STORE and bring your cotton and lumber to JOHN JOHNSON'S GIN AND MILL. Behind the stage were two classrooms. That, and the little library in the corner of the main room, provided for around ninety students in the four upper grades.

Two teachers handled all the classes. One served as superintendent and the other as the principal for all eight grades. One teacher had to be in the main room at all times, so that meant only one of the classrooms was in use.

The school offered sixteen subjects, all required for graduation. No electives. No honors club. No debate team. No organized sports or gym—just a dirt basketball court out front near the boys' and girls' outhouses. Then a spring junior-senior play, graduation ceremonies, and that was the works.

Even though the year ran from August to March, many students were out six weeks in August and September, going with their parents to pick cotton and live in migrant shacks in southeast Missouri. The teachers had to spend the next six weeks helping them catch up.

This was Arkansas, 1940. The Ozarks. Newton County. Judy. An isolated school in the poorest county of a state that habitually ranked at the bottom of all forty-eight states in educational standards. Add to this a political spoils system in which the teachers had no job security from year to year. Who was hired depended on who got elected to the school board. Election Day, sad to say, was a disgrace, with votes for school board and various county offices being bought right and left for a couple of dollars or a quart of moonshine whiskey. I'm not saying everybody sold his vote, or that vote selling was the decisive factor in every election. But any six-year-old could see what was happening.

Outsiders were not courted for teachers. The feeling was that the jobs ought to go to local people, so long as they had at least a couple of years of college and a teaching certificate. We called them by first names (they weren't old enough for "Aunt" or "Uncle"), and some by nicknames right in class. None of this Mr. and Mrs. or Ma'am or Sir business for our own folks.

One evening about twilight I was sitting in front of our store when Hudson's truck rolled up. Hilda Brown, one of the high school teachers, was in the cab with the driver. A bunch of my schoolmates came running from Lloyd's store and jumped on the flat bed. "Where ya goin'?" I asked.

"To a chicken roast at the creek."

I turned to my brother. "Tell Mama and Daddy I'm goin' to the creek with Hilda." Then I jumped on just as the truck was pulling away.

We rumbled down Route 123, twenty pairs of legs hanging off the sides, everybody singing and yelling. We passed our old house and the little hollow where I had led my brothers and sisters into the yellow jacket nest, then jolted to a stop at Ester Holt's. The house was dark.

Four big boys jumped from the truck bed and ran into the Pentecostal preacher's front yard. Then: "Squawk! Squawk! Squawk!" as they jerked chickens from the roost.

The four, each with a hen under his arm, leaped back on the truck. The truck rolled on, with feathers flying behind as the boys plucked the birds.

Two miles down the creek, the driver pulled off on a wagon road and halted beside a rock bar. The chickens were soon sizzling in frying pans over a hot fire.

"Ever'body grab a piece," one of the older boys said.

I bit into a leg and threw it into the creek. It was too tough to chew. I heard someone say, "This ole hen's got maggots!"

Hilda was offered a piece. She blushed in protest. "This isn't right. Nobody told me about this. We're all going to be in trouble."

Hilda's protests to the contrary, we hung around the fire an hour or two, joking about the chickens, kidding and punching one another and teasing our teacher. Then we left for Judy, with vows not to tell a soul.

Daddy and I left about five the next morning to buy a load of feed at Russellville. When he walked back into the store around two o'clock, Mama looked at me gravely. Howard Jean stood by, a grin of sweet anticipation on his face.

"Where did you go last night, James Carl? Don't lie, tell me the truth."

"J-just down to the creek with Hilda and a bunch from school. We fried a few chickens."

"Whose chickens?"

It was plain now that she knew. Somebody had squealed.

"Mama, I didn't know they were going to stop at Ester's house."

"Were you in on the stealing?"

"No, Mama. Honest to my grandma, I stayed on the truck."

Daddy got into the act. "Where'd you hear all this, Hester?"

"O.J. George told his folks this morning. It's all over everywhere. They're talkin' about it in Jasper. How these Judy kids stole a preacher's chickens. And with one of their teachers along."

"Mama, Hilda didn't even know the boys were goin' to get Ester's chickens."

"Did you know?"

"No, Mama. Believe me." I was in tears.

"What's being done about it?" Daddy asked Mama.

"The parents are making all the kids pay him. It comes to about fifty cents apiece."

Preacher Ester was then working at Johnson's mill, firing the boiler. Later that afternoon he stopped by our store. Daddy led me over to him.

"James Carl has somethin' to say to you."

I couldn't bear to look at him. I kept my eyes on the floor as I confessed, "I'm sorry about taking your chickens."

"Give him your money, Son," Daddy said solemnly.

I handed him a shiny new fifty-cent piece, money I had been saving for a fishing reel. "Thank you, James Carl," was all he said.

My classmate, Junior Johnson, had been working after school at his father's mill, helping Ester keep wood in the boiler. Junior didn't go to work that afternoon, or the next. The Johnsons lived in the cobblestone house straight across the road from our store. When I saw Junior finally come out, I yelled, "What's wrong? You eat the maggots?" Others picked up the remark, and for the rest of the year we called him "Ole Maggot."

Poor Hilda was so ashamed. She was teased even more than Junior. Frank Martin, who was older than Daddy, was one of those who never let her forget the chicken fry. Whenever he saw her in a group, he would catch her eye and crow like a rooster. Then haw-haw as Hilda blushed all shades.

I don't blame Hilda or any of my teachers for high school being a washout for me. They undoubtedly did the best they could under the circumstances.

Sure, I made a B average. With no incentive, it was just too easy. I stopped trying. I only took textbooks home for the weekend. This was because pie suppers and other community functions were held on Friday and Saturday nights, and Church of Christ services on Sunday. We were told not to leave anything in our desks.

My biggest problem was social maladjustment. My classmates were four years or more older than I. By the tenth and eleventh grades they were interested in romance. I could have cared less. I did enjoy intercepting love notes and stealing confession magazines which the girls kept in their desks.

The one boy I related to best was David Criner. Not because his great-great-grandparents and mine were brother and sister. Most of us in Judy High School were kin in some respect. We related because we were both so different from the rest.

David was a handsome fellow, wiry and strong, but limped from an attack of polio. He was also extremely shy and introspective. Teachers and classmates knew this and teased him about girls unmercifully. He could hardly say hello to a female without blushing.

David turned to books. A true intellectual, he loved to discuss war, history, politics, literature, the Bible—any subject. We spent hours together, sometimes arguing fiercely, other times just sitting and thinking, dangling our fishing poles over a deep hole, and saying nothing.

One Saturday morning, David and I were reclining on the porch of Gussie and Jeames' cafe, reviewing the latest war news.

"You boys know the meanin' of them big words yer usin'?" Jeames asked.

"Certainly," said David, who just happened to have a dictionary. "Look them up in here and ask us."

"I've got a better idea," Jeames said. "David, you take the dictionary and ask James Carl the meaning of a word. Then he'll ask you one. See who can set the other down the quickest."

The game started. An eleven- and a fifteen-year-old hurling jawbreakers at each other while the crowd kept building. This went on for quite a while. I forget who won, but I remember Jeames saying to me, "Son, you're a regular little professor."

The nickname stuck, except that it got shortened to 'Fesser."

My brother won his nickname about the same time. Cousin Lloyd observed him scrambling up a white oak tree and remarked, "That boy's a real possum." Somebody else said, "Lookit him hang from that tree limb. He's more like a monkey."

Monkey was whittled down to Monk. So Howard Jean and I became Monk and 'Fesser.

My brother did kind of look like a monkey with his burr head and animated ways. He was continuing to give Mama fits about school. That and worrying about Daddy going to war deepened the lines in her tired face. Daddy had received his draft notice to report to the induction center in Little Rock for his physical exam. "Taking a man with six kids isn't right," Mama sobbed. "Why couldn't they give him an exemption."

She looked at the clock. "Time to leave for school. Now where is that brother of yours? Howard Jean? Howard? Come out of your hiding place!"

She looked in all the usual spots, behind counters, under beds, and even beneath a pile of dirty clothes. "I'll bet he's gone off with the Greasy boys again," she said. The Greasy boys were from a large, poor family who lived in a shack above Judy. They were called this because of their oily hair. Mama didn't trust them, perhaps because the parents didn't keep their children in school.

Daddy came in from feeding the dogs, with Monk trailing after him. Monk saw Mama and started to run through the house. She grabbed him by the collar. "Wash the egg off your face and get ready for school, young man." Then, calling to the twins: "Hurry up, girls, so I can comb the rat nests out of your hair."

Much as I was bored with school, Mama never had to tell me. A few minutes later I looked back from the school steps and saw her pushing Monk up the path toward the grade school building.

She handed him over to a teacher at the door and turned her back to the store. Poor Mama didn't know he would be out the door or a window as soon as the teacher turned her back, and running to join Huck and Buck, the two Greasy boys nearest his age. They would spend the day on the creek bank, with Monk returning just before school let out so Mama would think he had been there all day.

It wasn't that easy when the teacher thought to keep a closer eye on him. In that event, Monk would toss a pebble or walnut at the far wall of the school room. When the teacher turned to investigate, Monk would jump up from his desk and run.

On days when escape was impossible, he spent much of the time with his nose in a ring at the chalkboard. His teacher always drew the ring high enough so that the troublemaker would have to stand on tiptoes. Wily Monk always carried chalk and an eraser in his pocket. When the teacher turned her head, he erased the ring and drew one lower to avoid the torture.

The day came when Daddy went off to Little Rock with a bunch of other inductees. Mama was so worried. She put groceries on the wrong shelves, made mistakes in addition, and broke down and cried a couple of times. Without a telephone, there was no way for him to call to tell us that he had passed or failed the physical. We simply had to wait until he got back or word came that he had been sent on to a camp.

If he failed, he would be coming back by bus to Harrison, and catch Cousin Noil Martin's mail truck that ran each day to Judy. Noil usually came about eleven, so every day I was standing on our store porch, watching for him to turn the corner. That Friday I was there and caught sight of Daddy. "Mama, Mama, Mama! He's back!" I screamed.

Daddy rushed into the store and hugged Mama. She was so tickled. She said happily, "Well, what'd they find wrong with you, Fred?"

Daddy looked embarrassed. It was hard for an Ozark man to admit he had a physical weakness. Finally he spoke, not loud enough to be heard by the men around the heating stove. "They said I have a hernia."

That was one of the happiest days of our life as a family.

Daddy continued with his grocery route, training dogs, and hunting. Mama, hard as she worked, would have been contented in the store, except for Monk.

Five days a week she had to walk him to school. Once he broke loose and climbed a power pole. "Mama, if you don't go back to the store and lemme alone, I'll te'ch this w'ar and 'lectrocute myself." Mama backed up, telling him, "When your Daddy comes home, he'll give you a thrashing."

Daddy made Monk dance a tune. But it did no good.

Mama caught on that he was stealing from the store. She started emptying his pockets every time he went out. Then she found he was holding change in his mouth. Once he swallowed a quarter to keep her from getting it. After that, every time he went to the outhouse, he looked for that quarter.

Mama bought punchboards for which the customer paid a nickel a punch for a chance to win a foot-long pecan bar. Monk took to sneaking the punchboard under his bed cover at night and shining a flashlight across the punch holes until he spotted a lucky number. The next morning he begged Mama for "just one little punch." When she gave in, he won a candy bar that lasted him all day on the creek.

She'd say, "You're the luckiest little boy I've ever seen. I don't understand it."

Monk was with the Greasy boys when school was in session. At other times his best friend was Junior Nichols, the son of Jeames and Gussie. "Nick," as Monk called him, didn't play hooky, but otherwise he was a bundle of charming freckled mischief just about to explode.

One year, around the first of December, Monk stole all the firecrackers Mama had ordered for Christmas sale. That night he and Nick sneaked up to the grade school's woodpile and planted explosives in knotholes and under loose bark. The next morning, for a change, Monk was in school. By chance, the teacher asked him and Nick to bring in a load of wood.

The two malefactors glanced knowingly at each other and pretended to be sick.

"All right, if you two aren't feeling well, I'll send Chip and Joe."

The other boys brought in the wood and put the sticks in the stove. Bang! The teacher jumped as if she had been shot. The stove lid shot up in the air. A moment later, another bang. Then another.

"Chip and Joe, march up here." the teacher demanded angrily. She drew two nose rings on the blackboard, while Monk and Nick almost collapsed in laughter.

The next load of wood brought the same results, and the next, until the teacher sent a crew to dig the firecrackers out. Only then did peace reign in Monk and Nick's classroom that December.

The two comrades in misconduct hunted together. One evening their dogs ran a skunk under some driftwood in Dry Branch on the far side of Graveyard Hill. Monk caught the animal and carried it back to Judy. They broke into the school and stowed the skunk in their teacher's desk.

The next morning both were on hand to see their teacher open her desk drawer.

"Spitttttttt! Spitttttttt!" The skunk leaped out, throwing spray in her face and running around the room in fright. "Get that animal!" she shrieked.

Monk and Nick were convulsing. Their guilt was plain to see. "You'll get a whipping—both of you," she screamed. "But first get that animal!"

Monk caught the skunk on the way out, with Nick right behind him. They didn't stop running until they reached the woods. The school stunk for a week. Both boys got hard whippings as soon as the superintendent got his hands on them.

Monk also had a knack for catching snakes. One morning he tucked one under his overalls, and to Mama's surprise went happily off to school. When the teacher came near, he said, "I brought a friend with me." The snake slithered out. The teacher screamed and ordered him to take his plaything and leave. That worked for several days until the teacher realized he was doing it just to get sent home.

With all his shenanigans, Mama gave Monk less credit than he deserved. "The Greasy boys put you up to all this meanness," she said repeatedly. "Stay away from them. they're bad, you understand. Bad." Each time, as soon as he could break away, Monk would head for the creek and his ragged friends.

To hear Mama, you'd think I was perfect. I loved it when she bragged on me before people. Mama just didn't know me very well.

A feisty little old lady we called Aunt Bell sat out in front of her tiny house across the road from our store. By this time I had a bike and I would race down the road straight at her, then at the last second, when she threw up her hands in fright, I'd turn the handlebars and skid around the corner.

Mama didn't whip me for this. I did it when she wasn't looking. When Aunt Bell or somebody else told her, I denied it with feigned innocence.

Then Aunt Bell came over one day and announced "James Carl stole my firewood."

Mama wouldn't accept that until she looked under the store porch and there it was. "See, I told you," Aunt Bell cackled. "Now what are ye gonna do about it?"

Mama grabbed the hickory limb she used on Monk and ordered me to bend over and pull up my britches' legs. I never thought Mama had it in her. She beat me until there were stripes. Aunt Bell went home grinning.

Then Mama learned I was innocent of that misdeed. My sister Loucille and David Criner's sister Mary had done it. Dear Mama was so contrite. "Forgive me, James Carl. I was wrong."

"Aw, I forgive you, Mama. Don't worry about it."

I've never forgotten that whipping. It was the only one she ever gave me.

Of course, she didn't know about the time I sneaked into the mill after quitting time and pulled the whistle rope and tied it down. It blew for ten minutes and could be heard for ten miles. Some thought a disaster had happened. Preacher Holt never left steam up in the boiler again.

After Daddy quit farming, Monk and I did not have enough to do, outside of school and even fishing and hunting, to occupy our time. That was true of all Judy boys whose parents had stores. We were expected to keep wood in the potbellied stove during the winter time. Occasionally, Mama let me tend the store when both she and Daddy had to be gone. That was when Monk played barber. He actually cut hair for a quarter a head.

My other major responsibility was to round up, every evening, our old brindle cow left over from the farm. That was no trouble. I had a brown shepherd mutt, naturally named Shep. All I had to say was, "Shep, go get Ole Bossy." The cow might be half a mile away and lying down in a ravine. Shep would find her, nip at her heels until she got up, and then drive her home.

Ole Shep was my beloved childhood pet. Daddy didn't keep hunting dogs long enough for me to get attached to them. Ole Shep was mine and he wasn't on the market.

The little booger was a scrapper. Charlie Jones had a little sawed-off, coal black bulldog named Nero. Every afternoon Shep and Nero battled at the back of our store. Shep won as many times as he lost.

Shep followed me fishing. He sat on the bank beside me, soulful eyes fixed on the line, waiting for his master to haul in a big 'un. I loved Ole Shep.

Monk's faithful four-legged companion was a coon named Ole Joe, which Daddy had captured as a baby.

Ole Joe rode on Monk's shoulder or trotted behind him to the creek and through the woods. Joe didn't care for dog or people food, but craved crawdads. Every morning Monk took him down to the little branch that ran behind the mill and let him forage for his breakfast. Ole Joe kept going further and further downstream. One morning he didn't come back and Monk thought he was lost. A year later Daddy's dogs treed a coon in a cave. Daddy looked in and saw Ole Joe with his collar still on him.

Daddy backed up the dogs and called, "C'mon out, Joe." The coon came. He remained with Monk several more years, then disappeared for good.

The state highway department started building a bridge on Route 123 across Big Creek. The workmen foolishly left several cases of dynamite unguarded in a cave. Monk took several cases and developed a new style of hunting.

Safely out of sight of parents and school, he'd head for the woods with his favorite hound dog, a shotgun, and a few sticks of explosives. When the dog chased a varmint up a tree and into a hole, Monk climbed up and planted the dynamite, lit the thirty-second fuse, and scurried back to the ground. The explosion blew the animal out and Monk finished it off with the shotgun.

Monk did not cuss, smoke, or chew. He would take a sip of moonshine only to get somebody else started. Once while hunting he came across four gallons of hidden moonshine. He carried the jars back and hid them in the Judy graveyard, about a half mile from the school. At noon he brought all of the ninth grade boys to the graveyard, showed them the whiskey, and said, "Drink up, fer we ain't got long." He managed to get the boys back into the school house. They began vomiting at their desks, and several even passed out.

Cousin Charlie, one of the teachers, recognized the problem and the culprit. He called Monk aside. "I know that you did this, Son. Take 'em back out and sober 'em up. If you bring me back a quart of whiskey, I won't say anything." To this, Monk agreed.

Monk led his charges back to the graveyard and ran them around the tombstones until they were levelheaded. But he failed to keep his promise on the moonshine. Cousin Charlie either forgot or decided it was better not to take the matter further.

I was long gone from Big Creek when Monk came to the end of the line at Judy School. He was twenty-one and in the twelfth grade when the superintendent, another cousin, called him in and said, "Son, you've been here long enough. It's time for you to get out. We're going to graduate you." They handed him his diploma at commencement. He could neither read nor write.

As for me, after having to retake the eighth grade, I completed high school in the standard four years. Starting with thirty-five freshmen, my class dwindled to nine seniors. David Criner was one of these.

School let out in March, three months before my fourteenth birthday. I was so short they had to put cushions on my chair so I could be seen during the graduation ceremony. I suppose my record still stands as the youngest student ever to graduate from Mount Judea High School.

Monk set a record as the oldest. He married a Newton County girl, moved to Kansas City, and went into business. Starting from scratch, he sold used cars and was soon making a hundred thousand dollars a year. One year, with Monk doing his own TV commercials, he and his partner sold twenty-two hundred cars.

On one he declared, "We finance anybody, from eighteen to ninety. Age makes no difference." How could he do this? "If you have a car that you've got $400 in, you ask $400 down," he said. "You can't lose."

Monk and I haven't seen much of each other over the years. Just family reunions and an occasional visit by me to Kansas City. Once I flew there to interview a professional football player. Howard (I've stopped calling him "Monk") insisted that he loan me a car. He met me at the airport in a gold-colored Cadillac. I felt like Elvis Presley driving down the street.

We were last together at a basketball game in Harrison. He sported a new hair style and looked much younger than his fifty years. We talked about old times. "I never did find that quarter I swallowed in the store," he said.

I felt no qualms about asking him about his shenanigans in school. He's always talked freely about his escapades.

"Why did you go to so much trouble to stay out of school?" I asked.

"I jist didn't like school. I'd rather go huntin' or fishin'."

"Mama was always bragging on me and fussing at you," I recalled. "Did you do some of that stuff just to get attention?"

"No, I reckon I was jist mean. Mama didn't like what I was doin', but she blamed the Greasy boys. She thought they wuz leadin' me wrong, when I wuz takin' *them* down the wrong trail."

"If you had it to do over again . . . ?"

"I don't know. Might be meaner. Might be better."

"When did you learn to read and write?" I asked.

"After I got to Kansas City, I saw educated fellers drivin' big Lincolns and Cadillacs. I figured if I was ever goin' to make any money, I'd better git crackin'."

We left the game and got into his new Lincoln. He was wearing a $10,000 Rollex watch with a solid gold band. I was driving a rented Ford Escort and wearing a K-Mart "blue-light" special.

On that trip I stopped in Jasper and visited around the courthouse. Garland Lee Bryant, the present county school supervisor, was a classmate of Monk's. We talked about my brother.

Declared Garland Lee: "He's one of a kind. There'll never be another Monk."

When I go to Judy, the old-timers still call me 'Fesser. When Howard Jean comes, they call him Monk. They remember me for one thing, my brother for another.

We don't look alike or talk alike. We share some values; in other respects we're poles apart.

With all our differences, I love him. I believe he loves me, too.

We're brothers, once together, and now far apart.

TEN
Fishing with the Judy Boys

Our fishing year started about the time school let out in March, when the cry rang through Judy: "The hornyheads are up!"

Monk grabbed a can, I picked up one of Mama's garden hoes (she still planted a garden in Judy), and we headed for Grover Greenhaw's barn lot where the juiciest and liveliest red worms nested under moldy cow manure. With a can full of wigglers, hooks, sinkers, and lines in our pockets, potato chips and two twelve-ounce bottles of Nehi root beer, we headed for the little fishing hole where Judy Branch empties into Big Creek.

Cousin Goober, Lloyd's son, had beat us there. "Whoopee! I got an eight-incher! Makes my four-teenth."

"Hot dog!" we heard Cousin Clyde yell. "Here comes my tenth."

By the time we cut two sycamore poles and strung our lines, a dozen Judy boys were lined along the bank. Monk dropped his worm in the swirling water and—zingo—he pulled out a hornyhead. The little rascal had three on his stringer before I caught my first.

I should explain that hornyheads are just overgrown slickhead bass minnows which turn the colors of a rainbow and grow little horny bumps on their heads as they swarm up the creeks and branches to spawn in early spring. For a couple of weeks they are ravenously hungry and will bite almost anything you wiggle before their noses. They rarely grow over eight inches, but they sure can arc a sycamore pole.

This cold Saturday morning in 1941 we jerked hornyheads until our arms were sore. Then Cousin Clyde started a fire, Monk hacked off fish heads, and Goober and I scraped away scales and sliced off fins with our sharp pocket knives. Cousin Billy Buck pulled one of his mama's big fry pans from a sack, rinsed it in the branch, dried the inside on his shirttail, dabbed in a hunk of lard, and hunkered over the fire. By the time the grease was hot, Goober and I had a batch of scaled hornies wrapped in flour and ready for frying.

Yum, yum, yum, before you could say Uncle Willie Pink picked a peck of pickled popcorn, we were feasting on fried hornies and crackers, swigging 'em down with root beer. Nothing tasted better on a frosty March morning.

By the time the hornyhead rush was over, thousands of thick-lipped, bottom-crawling, blue, red, and yellow suckers came surging up the creek to spawn. These fish ran up to four pounds and two feet in length. At the cry, "Suckers shoaling!" men and boys sharpened their gigs.

Gigging was illegal, but whoever saw a game warden on Big Creek in the early 1940s? Every able man and boy went sucker fishing.

We left Judy about sundown carrying gigs, a net, tow sacks to hold the fish, pine knots and strips of rubber chopped from old tires, and horse-muzzle sized wire baskets which would be tied on the end of thick sycamore poles to hold the rubber and pine torches.

By dark we were at the creek, the torches lit, and everybody in place. Daddy hollered, "Let's go, boys!" and the torchbearers and giggers splashed into the first shoal, chasing the fish downstream toward where the rest of us waited—with a net stretched across the upper end of the deep hole where the fish would seek refuge.

Standing where the current bulged the net backwards, forcing a natural trap, the cold, rushing water biting at my bare legs, I saw the small army of giggers coming. They were hollering and thrusting their three-pronged weapons at the elusive, dark shapes in the swift water. "Whooie! Take a look at this 'un!" Cousin Lonzo hollered, as he held up his gig to remove a writhing three-pound blue sucker and throw it to the bank where two teenaged boys carried sacks. "Yippee!" "Yeah!" others yelled as they speared big suckers against rocks.

"Whomp!" The first big sucker, driven down by the giggers, hit the pocket in the net. I grabbed him by the gills and tossed the fish to the rockbar where Cousin Clyde held a sack. "Whomp! Whomp!" Two more. "Whomp! Whomp! Whomp! Whomp!" As the giggers came closer, the suckers hit faster than I could throw them to Cousin Clyde.

We finished that shoal, walked around the deep hole, and hit the next shoal below. By nine o'clock we had three tow sacks full—around a hundred and fifty pounds of fish. L.R. "Crocket" Criner, David's brother, gave the signal as the giggers moved off the last shoal.

"Game warden coming! Game warden!" Crocket yelled, as others who were in on it took up the cry.

Cousin Leck, Uncle Elmer's oldest son, took off for the hills. He always did, every spring, every time the trick was pulled. The rest of us ran a little ways and came back to the creek. After awhile Cousin Leck came slipping sheepishly back and said, "Boys, you w'ar jist foolin'. There ain't no game warden."

There never was. The county game warden seldom set foot on Big Creek. And it was understood that as long as we gigged suckers, and not gamefish, we wouldn't be bothered. But Cousin Leck never believed that.

The suckers stopped running in April. We Judy boys had to find other means of amusement outside of school, until the bass began hitting about mid-May. We played horseshoes and marbles in front of the stores, with the usual dogs and occasional cows and hogs walking around us. We moved only for a car or truck. The north mail came in the morning, the south mail in the afternoon. The soda pop truck and grocery salesmen came on Wednesday, the grocery deliveryman on Thursday. That pretty well took care of Judy's motor traffic in a week.

On Saturday, Judy was crowded with families coming to mill and market. With nothing constructive to occupy our time, we turned to mischief. One Saturday we gave "hot foots" to the men lounging on the benches along the store porches. We stuck a comb tooth in a crack above a shoe sole, lit it with a match, and ran away before the unsuspecting victim felt the heat. Another Saturday we played cops and robbers with B.B. guns. We were the cops and any male who turned his back was a robber. We zinged a lot of rear ends before Uncle Loma, the constable, caught on to what was happening.

By May our parents were glad to see us back on the creek. Billy Buck, Monk, Goober, David, and I grabbed a minnow seine and headed for the slick rock shoals near the old Will Holt place. We caught a bucket of slickhead minnows and moved down to the Lyles' Bluff Hole, a mile further down the creek. This was in 1941, before we had rods and reels. We simply stood on the shallow side of the hole and pitched our lines into the deep water.

I tossed my bait toward the big boulder which anchored the middle of the hole. I felt the sinker touch bottom, jerked it a few inches, let it lay a minute, then jerked again.

"Zip!" An ole bass popped my line hard and ran with the bait. Easy, easy, I let him take a yard or two, then set the hook. He almost pulled the line from my hand. Keeping the line taut, I gave him a couple of yards, then started reining him in. He took a wide sweep upstream, circled back, then came running toward the bank. I pulled in line fast—and just in time—for he jumped. Had the line been slack, he would have likely thrown the hook. Instead, I kept his tail low on the water, and with one last flip, he surrendered.

Sixteen inches. Two pounds. Not bad for a creek brownie, the toughest fighter you'll ever engage.

We hung around the Lyles' Bluff till after dark and started home with our string. We arrived wet and soggy around 10:00 P.M., smelling like the dead fish we were carrying. Mama was in bed awake. Daddy was out coon hunting.

"James Carl? Howard Jean? Is that you?"

"Yes, Mama," we said.

"Put some dry clothes on. I'll get up and fix you something to eat."

"No, Mama, we'll just have baloney sandwiches and root beer and go to bed. Goodnight, Mama."

"You've got to have more than that." Up she came in her long white flannel nightgown to fry us some eggs. Not until we had eaten did she go back to bed. By then it was time for Daddy to come home from coon hunting.

The bass fishing tapered off in midsummer, then picked up again in August, about the time school started. School didn't worry Monk and the Greasy boys. David Criner and I waited until after school to head for the Tom Greenhaw Hole, which is just below some cold springs, and beside a high bluff under which the bass hide on hot muggy days when the water is low.

In August the crawdads shed their hard skins. We caught a bucket of softshells, then inched around the face of the bluff to a ledge hanging over the deep water. We hooked our crawdads through the tail, dropped them over the side, and watched them dart and dive to the deep bottom where they would back up under the bluff. Then we sat back to wait in the oppressive heat.

Ever so slightly, I felt a pull on my line. "Easy, easy," I whispered. "Mr. Bass is making up his mind." Then a hard turn. "Mustn't let him run too far. He'll hang me up under the bluff. Easy, easy. Now!" I set the hook and pulled straight up. In a minute, out he came, flouncing and fussing. I grabbed him by the gills and slid him on our stringer.

David caught three. I got two more, plus a monstrous goggle-eyed perch. Then we shucked our clothes and went for an icy swim. It was simply too hot to fish any longer.

We fished at night for catfish and eel on the sandbar across from the Tom Greenhaw Bluff. One evening Monk and I set out a long trot line, baited with live slickheads, across the lower end of the hole. Around ten o'clock Monk felt to see if anything was on it and hollered, "C'm hyar quick, 'Fesser. We've got a lolloper!" We had a stout line and it took us both to pull it out. When the first hook got close to the bank, Monk held out our dim lantern and squealed, "Eel!" He saw the second hook. "Anuther eel! Anutherin'! 'Fesser, thar's an eel on ever hook!"

I lifted up the line at the first hook. Having put down the light, Monk grabbed the first wiggling creature.

"Yech! Aw, yech! Hit ain't no eel. Hit's a six-foot water moccasin!"

We pulled out thirteen big moccasins—the nonpoisonous kind—big around as our wrists. In disgust, we cut off the hooks and let the moccasins keep them in their bellies.

A few evenings later we were hand fishing on that same sandbar when Monk got a powerful bite. "I've got a ten-pound cat, 'Fesser. I ain't foolin'. Hit's a shore nuff big 'un."

"Unh, unh, unh," Monk grunted. "I'm a bringin' it in."

He dragged it close to the water's edge, reached his hand for a gill, and jumped back. "'Fesser, hit's an ole snappin' turtle. Hit lak to bit my finger plumb off."

I turned on the light. Monk pulled the critter out on the sandbar. He stepped on its back and crowed, "Hit's big as a washtub. I can ride it. Whoopee!"

The turtle wasn't really that large, but it was the biggest I'd ever seen on Big Creek.

Somehow we got that turtle home.

The next morning after Mama opened the store we tied Mr. Snapper beside the front step. Aunt Bell came tripping along and started to step up. The turtle snapped at her foot. She jumped back in fright, "Lord have mercy! Lord help me! What is that creature?"

Mama came running and the ole turtle snapped at her. When she saw Monk and me holding our breath in glee, she knew where the guilt lay. "Get that thing, that awful thing away from here. Kill it. Take it off and bury it and don't let me see it again." Mama was really roused up.

Monk turned the turtle loose in Criner's pond.

When the fish weren't biting we could always find something interesting along the creek. One summer day in 1942, David and I were four miles down the creek and having no luck when he suggested we explore the Tony Barnes Cave. I had heard of the cavern, but never been in it. A dog was reported to have chased a fox into the mouth and come out days later on Cave Creek. No one, David said, had ever explored it to the end or checked the dog story out.

The mouth of the cave was hidden behind a thick growth of dogwoods just above the creek. We made a torch by filling an old horse muzzle full of dry pine chips and tying that to the end of a long pole. David lit the chips and we started on our great adventure, skipping along a narrow passage about eight feet high. After a hundred yards, the tunnel divided.

"We go to the right," David said. He drew an arrow on the floor at the juncture with the toe of his shoe, pointing the way back. Having just turned twelve, I tripped along beside him with no fear. After all, he was sixteen and had been in the cave before. Passages kept going off to the sides. At each juncture he marked an arrow to lead us safely back. I had never been this far back in a cave. What fun.

I was carrying the torch when we came into a big room. The floor was wet, indicating water close by. I was thinking that our pine chips were burning short when I tripped over a rock and lost my balance. The pole dipped in my hand, causing the wire basket to flip and empty the burning chips on the wet floor. In an instant we were plunged into near darkness.

"Grab what you can and let's go back," David shouted. I picked up two that were still burning. He managed to get hold of a couple. We started back at a trot. The chips were burning close to my fingers. Closer and closer. "David, I can't hold them any longer." I let them fall to the floor. A moment later he had to drop his. We were now in total darkness, at least a half mile from where we had gone in. It suddenly occurred to me that we had made no mention of going in that cave when we had left home. Nobody would know where to come looking for us. We were lost in the dark bowels of the mountain.

David struck a match. "Don't worry, I've got some more in my hat brim." We came to where the next passage split and tried to see an arrow. By match light we couldn't find the mark. "I think we go this way," David said and led the way.

Another match. Another junction. No arrow.

I didn't say it. David didn't say it. We both knew we were lost.

"I've got a few more matches left," David noted. "Then we can burn our clothes."

We'll die naked and starving in this cold dark place. We'll starve to death. I didn't whisper my worst fears, but David must have sensed my growing fright. "Remember we left our reels at the mouth of the cave," he said. "They'll know we went in here." *But what if nobody comes to the cave mouth for days?* I thought.

Then we rounded a corner and saw far ahead a thin sliver of light. "That isn't the entrance," David said. "Maybe. . . ." His voice trailed off. I knew he was thinking, "Is it big enough for escape?"

We had to stop, crawl, then worm our way along the cramped passage. I wiggled ahead. "Unh, unh." I twisted my shoulders, then my hips. "Unh." With a final squeeze, I was out.

I grabbed David's hand and pulled him through. Glory, hallelujah! We were out. Through an exit hardly big enough for a groundhog. It had to be a miracle.

I had nightmares for weeks. It was years before I could summon enough courage to enter another cave.

Every two or three weeks Daddy took us Judy boys fishing in his pickup to another stream. We went to the Buffalo River, or to Cave, Piney, or Hurricane creeks. This Friday, Crocket Criner, Junior Nichols, and Goober and Gander Hefley came along for an overnight to Cave Creek.

Goober's real name was Harold Dean. His brother Gander had the same name as me, James Carl Hefley. Goober was a little younger than I, and Gander a little older. They belonged to Cousin Lloyd, the postmaster, and were descended from Great-grand-pa Jim through my great-uncle Bill.

We netted a bucket of minnows and set up camp under a big overhanging bluff where pioneer settlers had once lived in a cliff house. A narrow grassy strip stretched between the bluff and the creek bank. An ideal place to tumble and wrestle and lie in the grass holding our lines.

We pitched out our baits and waited an hour without a nibble. The sun was dropping over the mountain behind us when Daddy and L.R. put our supper together, while the rest of us horsed around in the grass. We ate. Dark came, and still no bites. Daddy had brought along a dog, and he went down the creek looking for a coon. Gander, Crocket, Goober, and Junior flopped on an old quilt spread under the bluff and played cards. After awhile they fell asleep, leaving Monk and me to fish.

I tossed my bait far out in the darkness, heard a telltale splash, and felt a soft drag on the line indicating the hook and sinker were sinking to the bottom. A few minutes later I sensed a slackness and started pulling the line in. Near the bank the line turned upward. "Shine the light," I asked Monk.

The line led to the top of a willow where a snake held my minnow in its mouth! "Nobody will ever believe this," I said to my amazed brother.

I jerked the line free and tied on another hook and sinker. A bullfrog began sounding off nearby: "Harumph! Harumph! Harumph!" "Catch 'em, Monk, before he wakes the guys up."

Monk sneaked up behind the frog and shot out a hand as fast as you can blink and grabbed that frog.

"Lemme have 'em," I said. "I read in a sporting magazine that you can catch a lunker bass on a bullfrog."

I clipped my hook through the old frog's chin and tossed him out in the water. He hit with a mighty splash.

We settled back again, the only sounds the snoring from the pallet under the cliff behind us. Finally I said, "Looks like that big bass isn't interested." I started pulling my line in and again it was slack.

I kept pulling in my line. "Something took it back to the bank. Aw, shucks, it's jist my ole frog. He swam all the way back and is sittin' right here beside me." Monk was laughing so hard he was about to roll into the creek.

Junior woke up and had to hear about the snake and the frog. He laughed as hard as Monk. "Well, 'Fesser cain't say he ain't caught nuthin'," he said.

Monk and Junior quieted. With all of our lines baited in the water, we fell asleep. Around 2:00 A.M. I was awakened by a swishing in the grass. My line was going out fast. I caught it just in time and pulled out a snapping turtle that would weigh at least twenty-five pounds.

Monk and Junior jumped up to see what had happened. "You can have 'em," I said. "I'm going back to sleep."

Monk dragged the turtle around behind Crocket, Gander, and Goober, and back under the bluff. "Put the turtle in bed with 'em," Junior suggested.

"Nah, he'll eat 'em up," Monk replied. "We'll cut off his head and then throw 'em in th'ar bed."

Junior took a butcher knife, brought to clean fish, and sawed on the turtle's rough neck while Monk held up the head with the fishing line. Junior was down to the last slip of skin when the line broke. Neck severed and hanging by the skin, the gory creature waddled by instinct toward the creek, blood spurting, straight toward the pallet on which Crocket, Gander, and Goober lay.

"Hey, hey!" Gander snorted. "What are you boys doin'? Hey, git that thing away. Look out, Crocket! Move Goober!" Crocket and Goober awoke just in time to roll and dodge the stream of blood as the turtle plodded painfully across their bed and on to the creek.

Gander hollered at Monk and Junior as they ran away. "You boys did this. We'll git you!" Shrieking and howling with glee, they disappeared down the creek.

The fall of '42, Goober and I got rods and reels. We practiced casting into a bushel basket in his yard, moving the basket a few feet further away after a hit.

His mama's chickens kept getting in our way, so we put corn on our hooks and started teasing the fowl. Before Goober could jerk his away, a big plump hen swallowed corn, hook and all, and took off squawking. His mama came running. "What 'er you boys doin'? Oh, my, you've caught one of my hens!" Goober and his mama went running after the chicken, Goober winding on his reel to pick up the slack line while I stood back, busting my sides. They caught the old hen and had her for supper.

Rods and reels meant artificial bait, which fishermen call plugs. We quickly learned what plugs were best for the seasons: yellow bees with spinners in late spring when the water was murky; minnow imitators, like the Heddon River Runt, in early summer; and top-water plugs, such as the Jitter Bug, in later summer when insects were falling from tree limbs over the water.

The best time of day for plugging on Big Creek came about dark or a little after when bass came out to feed at the shallow upper and lower ends of the big holes. The first man to throw his plug in usually got the strikes.

The best stretch of creek ran from the Tom Greenhaw Bluff to the Lizzie Eddings Hole just above where Big Creek ran into Buffalo River. You couldn't cover it all in one night, so we took the upper half one time and the lower half the next. The idea was to be first at each hole.

One evening in late August 1943, Goober and I fished the upper holes. We reached the Henry Hensley Hole, near Route 123, a half hour after dark, making our first casts ten feet back from the water's edge. Suddenly we heard another reel whirl close by, then two men talking. Outsiders! We could tell by their accents.

We sneaked closer and heard one say, "We'll take that big bluff hole down the creek next." Then they walked over to their big Buick left parked beside the road.

They were heading for Lyles' Bluff, the top producer on the creek. We couldn't let them get there first.

"Let's beat 'em, Goober!"

Lickety-split, we flew across the rock bars barefooted, splashing through shoals, eyeing the car lights as the outsiders moved along the winding road. They beat us there by a whisker and parked on the deep side of the hole where boulders and heavy undergrowth made it difficult to cast.

We raced in from the shoal side, hurling our Jitter Bugs into the shallow upper end before coming to a complete stop. Glub, glub, glub. I could hear my bug talking as I retrieved it slowly across the water. Suck! A bass pulled the bait under. I set the hook. "Kersplash!" I hauled out a big smallmouth, dancing on his tail. "Suck! Kersplash!" Goober had one too!

The outsiders knew we were here by now. A high beam smacked me in the face. "Cut that light!" I yelled and tossed my Jitter Bugs out again. "Suck! Kersplash!" another bass. Goober caught a second, then a third. The outsiders were not only stupid, but angry, shining lights all around and cussing us loudly. Goober and I picked up our fish and walked off cackling.

The most difficult place to fish was the Lizzie Eddings Hole, far down the creek. Being wide and long, a boat was needed, which we didn't have. You simply could not cast far enough from the bank.

Only Monk could handle this hole. This is the way he did it: He filled his mouth full of crawdads, and holding his rod and reel above the water he quietly swam to the middle of the hole. There he baited his hook, cast out with his right hand, caught a bass, reeled it in, and strung it on one finger of his left hand, all while he treaded water. He didn't swim back to shore until his mouth was empty or he had five fingers full of bass on his left hand. Honest to my grandma, that's how he did it.

Every stream has its legendary fish, and Big Creek was no exception. Ole Alphin Brau (named for a beer advertised on KWTO, Springfield), a big lineside widemouth bass, lurked in the Lyles' Bluff. I saw him once, and to my eyes he looked a yard long. Well, at least two feet, with stripes as wide as my hand. Well, at least an inch across. I dangled a softshell crawdad right in front of his nose and he didn't even blink.

Ole Alphin Brau got bigger every year. He broke half a dozen lines every year. Nobody, not even Monk, ever caught him. I suppose he is still there, waiting for the lucky fisherman.

The wildest, roughest, and fastest stream in Newton County is Richland, some twenty-five miles south of Judy. Richland was reputed to be a moonshiner's paradise and a locale for others hiding from the law. Daddy hunted there occasionally and told us about the waterfalls and the deep blue holes beside the highest cliffs in the county. Monk and I begged until he agreed to take us fishing there.

We followed an old timber road to a "low water" bridge built by the forest service and chugged along an old wagon trace to where the ruts faded out in the woods. From there we walked to where the creek was surging over a slope of limestone and shale. We followed the slope to what looked like a small, crystal clear, pristine lake.

Monk and I catwalked around the wooded right bank to where he could climb out on a big oak leaning far out over the water. "I see 'em! I see 'em!" he shouted.

"Where?"

"There." He dropped a stick. The water swirled where it hit. He broke off another dead branch. A second swirl. " 'Fesser, they're hittin' anythang that moves!"

The hole was too wide and shallow at the upper end for casting. Daddy, Goober, and Billy Buck came around to where we were. After getting hung up in the bushes a couple of times, I finally managed to flip a live minnow under the leaning tree. A long, skinny bass took it immediately. "That 'uns starved to death," Daddy said when he saw it.

Monk pitched in his line and caught a twin to mine. Daddy and the other boys got into the action. By sundown we had over thirty long, slim bass on our stringers.

The next time we left before sunup. Daddy dropped Goober and me at the bridge and drove around the mountain and back to a crossing nine miles down the creek. Goober and I would walk downstream casting and meet him there.

The going was slow and rough, the scenery fantastic. We climbed up and down giant boulders amid which the water cascaded and formed small deep boiling pools. The water looked perfect, but we caught a bass only every mile or so. The snakes were plentiful, however. We saw at least thirty deadly poisonous cottonmouth moccasins. About four miles downstream we discovered the reason for the scarcity of bass: the creek was pouring over a cliff, which only the hardiest fish could ascend.

We climbed down and made our way around to a rockbar fronting on the deep hole at the foot of the waterfall. Goober cast a River Runt into the spray and hooked a fighting black smallmouth. I caught a couple. Then we pulled off our clothes and swam back into a cave behind the falls.

Fishing below the falls was better, but the going was no easier. We arrived at the rendezvous point as the sun was going down, legs and arms aching, shins and shoulders black and blue from slipping and sliding on rocks. We had only enough strength left to eat and flop into the truck for the bumpy ride home.

I made that Richland hike at least once a summer for the next seven years. The next time I returned with my nineteen-year-old city bride, Marti.

I believed my family would accept her, even though she was an outsider. I was sure she would charm them all, but I was fearful of tricks that might embarrass or frighten her.

When we drove into Judy, the whole crowd, Mama and Daddy and my brothers and sisters, plus several cousins, aunts, uncles, and hangers-on, came to see her get out of the car. By this time, Mama and Daddy had two more "young'uns": "Baby" brother John Paul, nine; and baby sister Patsy, only two.

John Paul walked boldly up to Marti and introduced himself as "James Carl's little brother." Then he reached into his pocket and uncoiled a four-foot king snake. "Hyar's a present for you, Marti." Monk stood by grinning.

Marti smiled sweetly at him. "Thank you, Johnny. May I hold your pet?" Whereupon she took the snake, wrapped it around her arm, caressed the reptile, and handed it back. "Keep it in your pocket for me."

Johnny's mouth hung open. Monk dropped his grin. The rest were staring at my Yankee wife as if they couldn't believe it. Finally Mama broke the ice and gave Marti a hug. "He didn't mean you any harm. Howard Jean put him up to it."

Early next morning the gang got ready for the annual trip to Richland. I wanted to show them I was still tough enough to make the hike. "No more than six or eight men or boys have ever made that trip," I crowed to Marti.

"Has a woman ever tried it?" she asked matter-of-factly.

"Nope," Daddy said, as if that ended it.

"Then I think I'll go."

Mama's face clouded. "Marti, you're not serious!"

"Why not?"

"Marti, you could get snake bit or fall and hurt yourself. They won't look out for you."

Daddy wasn't getting into an argument. All he said was, "We'd better be on our way." I'm sure he expected her to back out when we got to the first jumping-off place.

When we reached the little bridge we could see that Richland Creek was unusually high and swift. I looked at the boys. "Anybody goin' with me?"

"I ain't," Monk said.

Marti was getting out of the truck. "I guess it's just you and me," she said. "Won't that be romantic?"

"Marti, you'd better not," Daddy warned. "One of the boys will go."

"I'll be OK." She smiled confidently.

Daddy, reluctantly, left us there. Eight hours later we arrived at the lower crossing. Marti was black and blue, bruised and sore from the current banging her against rocks. Why had I been so dumb to let her come along?

She didn't seem to be the least bit regretful. "I made it," she said as she collapsed.

I looked around at the admiring glances. "Well," I said, determined to make the best of it, "now you know why I picked her."

ELEVEN
Grandpa Pulliam

My very favorite grandparent was Mama's daddy, Grandpa Pulliam Foster.

Except for Mama and Daddy, I felt closer to him than anyone else. He never had any money, yet my Grandpa Pulliam with a ho-ho-ho was the nearest real person to Santa Claus I ever knew.

He and Grandma Barbara lived miles from the nearest wagon road. I doubt if he ever had over ten dollars to his name. Wearing a tattered cap, an old shirt, and patched overalls, he often looked like he had just climbed out of a brush pile. Yet, to me, this dear old fellow was the strongest, bravest, smartest, kindest, and best man in the world. Except maybe my daddy. He was my favorite Grandpa and I loved him.

Now I'll have to back up a ways to when we were living in the log house five miles up the creek from Judy. Grandpa and Grandma Foster at that time lived far over on Honey Creek, so far that we didn't see them very often.

It was a good day's trip there. We would walk down Big Creek two miles, with Mama and the little ones riding Ole Babe, take a long turn up rugged Dry Creek, then climb the steep mountain and pass through the Rock Gap, a crevice in the bluff just wide enough for Ole Babe to shoulder through. From there I ran the rest of the way, down the sled road toward the sweet water spring that gushed out of a rock a hundred yards from their barn. By this time Grandpa Pulliam's dogs were barking, and with him still able to hear a little, he came running to meet me there.

"James Carl," he'd say, "ya've growed a foot sinct I seed ye." Then he'd squeeze my arm. "And feel that muscle! Ye're as stout as a young painther.

"James Carl, ye come jist at the r'at time [I always did, according to Grandpa]. There's two big blue-bellied lizards a sunnin' themselves on the rail fence jist past the house," he reported when I arrived for this visit. "Jist waitin' fer ye to knock 'em off with yer beanflip. I see ye've got hit with ye, fer hit's stickin' out of yer hind pocket."

Grandma, with her poor eyesight, had trouble making out which of her children's families was coming until she got close enough to hear voices. "Hester, ye've been ridin' a long time," she told Mama, when she realized who we were. "Let's git ye and them babies in the house whar hit's warm."

"Bring in some stovewood, Pulliam," she called back over her shoulder. "Th'ar all mighty hungry."

First things first for Grandpa. He knew I was more interested in the blue-bellied lizards. Ignoring Grandma, he led me ahead to the rail fence that started just past their log house. "There's a big 'un, James Carl. Try this little rock on 'em." I loaded my beanflip, took careful aim, and *zingo,* off tumbled the lizard.

"James Carl, ye're a crack shot. Right down yander is the 'tuther 'un."

I reloaded, took aim, and . . .

"Pulliam! Pulliam!"

"Now look what ye've done, Sis, ye've skeered our boy's lizard off." Everybody called Grandma Sis, except her children and grandchildren.

"Fergit that lizard, the both of ye. Air ye bringin' in that stovewood, 'er do I have to git it myself?" Grandpa winked at me and said slyly, "You wait hyar while I git the wood. Then we'll find that ole lizard."

He took the wood in, came back out, and we located the lizard. I cut another tiny notch in my sling shot's stock. Little notches were for lizards, big ones for birds and ground squirrels. Grandpa always called a sling shot a beanflip. He showed me how to make my first one. You slice two strips of rubber, each about a foot long and a half inch wide, from an old inner tube. Cut a fork with prongs about three inches long from a hickory bush. Notch each prong near the top, lap the end of a rubber strip over each stump, and tie tightly with a string that bites into the notch. Then you cut holes in the sides of an old shoe tongue and tie on the other ends of the strips. You hold the bottom of the forked stick in one hand and the shoe tongue in the other. Slip a marble-sized rock into your ammunition sack—the tongue; draw back, stretching out the rubber strips, and take aim. Then let the ammunition sack go, and out flies the rock. Look out blue-bellied lizard, ground squirrel, or any creeper of that size!

Grandma called us to supper. Fried squirrel, flour gravy, hot biscuits, and fried fruit pies, which was her specialty. Afterward Grandpa gave me a story by the big fireplace. He was wading into his second yarn about a panther on the mountain when Mama and Grandma decided it was bedtime. Daddy was out running his dogs, and Grandpa would soon join him.

After breakfast the next morning I saw Grandpa getting out his double-bit ax and crosscut saw. "Me and yer daddy air goin' to clear new ground. You can come along if ye stay out of the way."

"No, James Carl, you'd best stay here," Mama said, with Grandma nodding behind her. I was only about seven then. "You might get hit by a tree." Mama and Grandma always saw me and Grandpa Pulliam as an accident about to happen.

"Aw, let the little feller go, Hester. His daddy and me will look out fer him," Grandpa promised. Then, without waiting for permission, Grandpa pulled me out the door. I heard Mama and Grandma complaining behind us, with Grandma saying, "If that young'un gits kilt by a tree, you men will be the blame."

Clearing new ground may look like fun on "Little House on the Prairie." But it's hot, hard work. Cutting the trees is just the beginning. Next the limbs are slashed off with an ax and heaped in a brush pile for burning. Then the logs are snaked out by mule to be cut and split into firewood. Stumps have to be pulled and, if they're too deep-rooted, sawed or hacked off close to the ground. I didn't get scratched on that trip, although Grandpa and Daddy had to holler at me a few times. I even helped pile up the brush, and Grandpa let me start the fires. By sundown we had a half dozen piles afire across the hillside.

We came back to the house sweaty and grimy, with leaves and ashes blown into our hair by the wind. Just as we were sitting down to supper, a "Yahoo!" came from out beyond the spring. "More company's a comin'," Grandpa chortled. "Should be Leathy [Mama's sister] and Vester."

With Grandma fussing for everybody to stay at the table, Grandpa and I jumped up and ran to meet them. Utah and his little sister, Loucille, were with them. Utah—his mama named him for Utah Carl, the hero of a western ballad—was a year younger than me. A little sawed-off redhead with a crooked grin, he was a bundle of mischief. Utah and I always had a good time—and with Grandpa, no telling what might happen.

By the time we got back to the house, Grandma and Mama had squeezed in more plates. Utah and I finished before the rest. I couldn't wait to get him outside and show him a couple of leftover matches. "Grandpa let me start the fars," I said gleefully.

"I wanna see," Utah requested. Off we ran up the hill and stopped in a thicket about a hundred yards above the house. I looked back to see if anybody had followed us. "Go on, James Carl, I double dar' ye."

I looked back again, then ripped a match head across a flint rock and threw it into a pile of leaves.

Utah piled on more and pretty soon the thicket was crackling and smoke billowing above the treetops. We began backing up from the heat, Utah grinning and me starting to tremble a bit. "*Ye* did it, James Carl," he said.

I didn't feel proud at all. Now frightened, I broke off a tree limb and started beating at the flames. "*Ye* did it," he repeated. "Yes, I did it, but get a limb and help me put it out." I scowled.

That's when Utah ran off. To the house, I suppose, for pretty soon I heard Daddy yell, "Them boys have set the woods on f'ar." He and Uncle Vester and Grandpa came running and started beating at the burning leaves.

When the job was done, Uncle Vester and Daddy wanted to give it to us good. "Aw, they didn't mean no harm," Grandpa protested. "You won't do it a'gin, will ye boys?" I nodded fearfully, but all Utah said was "James Carl did it."

That was all anybody said until we got back to the house. Mama, Grandma, and Aunt Leathy lit into us like we had burned the house down. All while Grandpa kept saying, "They're jist little boys. They won't do it a'gin." And Utah, "James Carl did it."

I never did it again.

We worked all week and cleared at least two acres. Friday night we celebrated by going 'possum hunting. Utah and I climbed a persimmon tree and shook two of the little varmints out. Grandpa had a tow sack open and they fell right into it.

Despite the fire incident, it was a good week. Sixteen blue-bellied lizards, two 'possums, and Grandpa's Ole Blue treed a coon which Daddy shot off a limb. And we had a lot of fun times with Grandpa. I wanted to stay the next week, but Mama and Daddy said we had to head for home. Leaving wasn't so bad, since Grandpa and Grandma said they would be over to see us in about a month.

Grandma Barbara, as I noted before, was the daughter of Doctor Simon Solomon Sutton, who took care of sick folks on the Other Creek. Grandpa's folks lived in Boone County. His daddy, William Thomas Foster, was a railroad man who had followed the tracks from Chattanooga, Tennessee, where my Grandpa Pulliam was born. Grandpa Pulliam's ears had been damaged by a fever when he was young. Working on the railroad with his daddy and brothers had made his hearing much worse.

Grandma couldn't see well and Grandpa was about three-fourths deaf, even when I was a little boy. They had two big old steer horns to help them communicate long distance. Grandpa had one to call his dogs. Grandma used the other to call Grandpa in from the field to dinner. Grandpa also had an old conch shell which somebody brought him from the ocean. He could hear the roaring in it and would pass it around for us to listen.

Grandpa and Grandma Foster had seven children, four girls and three boys, less one boy born dead. Mama said he was easy on the boys but very protective of his girls. About the only place he would let them go, besides to kinfolks, was to Holiness meetings at the Dry Creek School House. Grandpa himself didn't attend church. When Grandma asked him to go, he'd say, "Go on, Sis. They've got 'nuff to worry about without havin' me thar."

Because he was so protective of his girls, they had to slip around and meet their boyfriends. Grandpa usually didn't know they had been courting until they were married. Then he insisted that they live in the weaning house nearby for several months.

Grandpa had his faults. He snorted moonshine and chewed tobacco. He cussed his mules until Grandma had to go out and shame him to be quiet. He let Ole Caterwaul, the county outlaw, sleep in his barn. And to hear some of his kin talk, he gave things away which he shouldn't have. If a man came by and asked—no matter how triflin' and lazy he was known to be—Grandpa might give him a bushel of potatoes. He just couldn't turn anybody away, which may help explain why he was dirt poor all his life.

The sight of Grandpa and Grandma coming up the trail to our house brought whoops of delight from me. When company came I had to sleep at the foot of my parents' bed. Howard Jean and the twins were put on a pallet. Daddy's feet smelled awful, especially in the wintertime when he didn't pull off his shoes to wade the creek. I hated to see grown-ups come unless they had kids. Except for Grandpa Pulliam.

With Grandpa around, every day was an adventure. First thing in the morning we were off to check my rabbit trap—a length of hollow log, baited with berries or nuts, closed tight at one end and open at the other, with a board shutter positioned above and hooked to a trip string. Grandpa was always sure I had a bunny. If I didn't, then one would take the bait the next night.

On one of his visits Grandpa taught me to make a box elder whistle. You cut a small limb about as long and thick as a man's forefinger. You hold it by the bark and tap the core loose with a sharp rock or the head of a sixteen-penny nail. You notch a hole near one end of the core and whittle off the top to make a little tunnel underneath. Then you slip the bark back on and blow to your heart's content.

I was about seven when Grandpa saw me trying to whistle with my lips. "Pucker and leave a hole jist big enough to let a little air out. Then puff," he said.

That's what I was doing the next day when Clara Kent gave me a whipping in school.

I came home from school puckering and puffing and whistling. Grandpa was sitting on our porch whittling. "What kind of bird is that? Hey, it's James Carl. He's a'whistlin' like a mockin' bird. I knew he could."

Mama came out as she always did to ask what had happened in school that day. When I looked kind of sly-like at Grandpa, she knew I had been in trouble. "What was it, Son?"

"Aw, I jist got a whippin' for whistlin'. I was only learnin' how."

"That's right, he wuz jist learnin', Hester," Grandpa broke in. "I cain't understand why he had to git a whippin' for jist whistlin' a little." But Mama and Grandma didn't see it that way.

Before Grandpa left, we went fishing his way. He never needed a hook and line. He went under the rocks and the banks with his bare hands and came out with bass, perch, turtles, and sometimes a big mottled brown water moccasin. "This old snake won't hurt ye," he'd say, holding the big wiggler just behind the head. Just the same, I backed off.

Grandpa carried a long stick with a prong at one end. On this particular morning we heard a whirring sound behind a cedar bush. "Oh, ho! An ole rattler," Grandpa chortled. Cat-footed, he slipped around the cedar. I hung back in fright. Mama and Daddy had told me to always get away fast from a rattler, a cottonmouth, or a copperhead. Don't even look at one cross-eyed.

"Thump." "Heh, heh, got the old booger. Hold still, ye rascal." I peeked around and there was Grandpa holding the rattler's head down with the forked end of his stick and reaching for a rock with his other hand. "Don't get near this 'un, James Carl. He's got a mouth full of pizen." Grandpa chunked the rock hard on the snake's head. One less rattlesnake.

After we moved to Judy, Mama became increasingly concerned about her aging parents. Grandpa's hair was turning to silver. Grandma looked so frail you'd think a hard wind might blow her away. His deafness was worse and so were Grandma's eyes. Mama worried that Grandpa might hurt himself with a gun or an ax and Grandma couldn't see to help him. And that Grandma might have an accident, and Grandpa couldn't hear her cry. Also, Mama said, with their being way over on Honey Creek, one of them would be dead by the time a doctor got there.

Mama wanted them to move over to Judy. Grandpa said he wasn't livin' in town where he couldn't have his mules and raise corn and tobacco. Mama, as you'd guess, eventually got most of her way. When I was twelve, she persuaded Grandpa and Grandma to let her sell their place to the Forest

Service. She took the money, a thousand dollars, and bought them a little four-room frame house and a few acres on the road at the top of the mountain, between Big Creek and Cave Creek. They had the prettiest view of anybody in Newton County. You could look out one window and see Cave Creek and cross the house to the other window and gaze upon Big Creek Valley. There was a spring in the bluff above their house, permitting Grandpa to pipe water down the hill and into the yard. You could say that Grandpa and Grandma Foster had the first "running water" in our part of the county.

We'd travel that way going fishing on Cave Creek. Grandpa Pulliam loved to go with us. Only he wouldn't fish with a line or reel. He'd grub around the banks and rocks with his hands, catching fish, turtles, and snakes as he always had. Even if we didn't have any luck with our fancy rods and reels, he'd always get something.

Poor ole fellow got to where he could hardly hear thunder. He'd just sit home and wouldn't even come to Judy. "Cain't hyar nobody," he'd say. "I'd jist be in the way." He'd stay up on the mountain and tend to his tobacco and corn, plow a little in his garden, and keep wood cut and stacked on his porch to be ready for winter.

He could read a little, but not enough to understand a newspaper. He couldn't write much more than a hen scratch. He was practically shut off from the world, except his eyes were still good. That and Grandma being able to hear kept them surviving.

His happiest times came when his grandchildren spent the night on the mountain. While Grandma puttered around in her little kitchen, he got out his checkerboard for a few games. Nobody, in my memory, ever beat him playing checkers, which proves he had a good mind. "It's yer move, James Carl," was about all he would say. That and "Looks lak I've got ye closed out. Let's have anuther game."

After I went to college, I always tried to visit him on trips home. I could tell he was going fast. He complained that the roaring in his head was louder and that he got dizzy trying to plow his garden. Still he wanted to play checkers and then go fishing. But he wouldn't beg to go along. You'd have to invite him. He didn't want to be in the way.

Once I didn't see him for a year. Then I came home eager to hit the creek with Daddy, Howard Jean, and the gang. It was late in the summer. Big Creek was pretty well fished out, they said. We'd try on Cave Creek.

"Can we take Grandpa Pulliam?" I asked.

"He cain't walk fifty yards without falling down," Daddy said. "A body has to keep close to 'em every minute."

"I still want him to go."

"You'll have to stay with 'em. You won't git in much fishin'."

"Let's take him. I'll watch out for him."

Daddy shrugged his okay. Daddy loved Grandpa, but he saw him fairly often and kind of took him for granted.

Grandpa beamed when we stopped to pick him up. Grandma fussed like an old setting hen and predicted all sorts of dire things would happen "If'un you'uns take this pore ole sick man." Grandpa was going if he had to be carried to the truck.

We drove down into Cave Creek valley, netted a bucket of bait minnows from a spring branch, then headed down an old logging road that paralleled the creek. The road ended at the creek about two miles from where the creek flows into Buffalo River, and we got out and walked to the water. With a little leading, Grandpa made it from the truck to the creek.

The others left Grandpa and me beside a rocky shoal where the water was running fast, bubbling and foaming, but still very shallow and not a bass to be seen. Saying he had to rest, Grandpa plopped down on a flat rock. I stood there beside him, watching Daddy, Howard Jean, Billy Buck, and Goober head downstream where the good fishing was supposed to be. I looked at the few minnows left us in a small bucket and wondered what good they would be.

They were barely out of sight when Grandpa got to his feet and announced he was feeling much better. "Jist the sight and smell of the creek stirs my blood," he said. Nevertheless, I kept a sharp eye out as he proceeded to wade into the water and began poking his hands under tree roots that extended into the creek. He pulled out a turtle, a frog, a couple of water moccasins, and a little catfish, before he waded back to rest.

"Hain't ye gonna fish any, James Carl?" He pointed to a boulder about ten feet wide in the middle of the shoal. "See the water goin' under and comin' out below. Mou't be an ole bass under that rock. Plunk a minner down and let it warsh under. Never kin tell."

Disbelieving, I waded out to the boulder. Indeed the water was flowing under it. I dropped my bait into the creek and let the current pull it underneath.

Wham! The rod almost jumped out of my hand. I jerked back and felt a quivering on the end. I reeled out a two-pound bass.

"Didn't I tell ye, James Carl?" Grandpa chuckled from his resting place.

I strung the fish and waded back. I caught another bass and another and another until the stringer was full. There was evidently a sort of cave under the rock and it was teeming with bass.

Late in the afternoon, Daddy, Howard Jean, and the cousins came dragging back. They were soaked to the skin from wading in deep water, and bone tired. Billy Buck carried their catch, two little skinny bass on the stringer clipped around his belt. "Don't suppose you fellers caught many either," Daddy said.

Grandpa hadn't heard a word, but he understood their thoughts. "James Carl's got a little 'un or two on his stringer here."

Proudly I lifted up our catch. Their eyes bugged. "Where'd you get 'em?" Daddy asked.

"Grandpa caught 'em with his bare hands."

I could see they doubted.

"OK, you still won't believe me, but we caught every one from under that big rock." I don't think they believed me then, either. I've never been back to that boulder. I've never found a fishing place like it since.

That was Grandpa's last fishing trip. His health kept worsening until he couldn't get out of bed. I saw him the last time in March 1962. His hair was thin and ghostly, his cheeks sunken. But the old twinkle was still in his eyes.

I yelled at the top of my voice: "REMEMBER THAT TIME WE WENT FISHING ON CAVE CREEK?"

He moved his head in a weak nod and smiled.

"WE REALLY CAUGHT SOME BASS, DIDN'T WE?"

"W-e s-h-o-r-e d-i-d, J-a-m-e-s C-a-r-l." He couldn't lift his head.

Two weeks later Mama called to say he was dead. The funeral notice said he was seventy-eight years old.

The next year Grandma tripped over a dog and broke her hip. From then on everything went downhill until she joined Grandpa.

The day after I wrote this chapter, my oldest daughter, Cyndi, dropped by with her two children. "Pa, go fishin'," her three-year-old Joshua begged.

I had been meaning to take Josh. I had taken Jessica, his five-year-old sister, a couple of times, but never Josh. A pile of work was on my desk. I started to beg off, but he persisted: "Pa, go fishin'. Take me."

I couldn't withstand those pleading eyes.

We drove about thirty miles from Chattanooga, where we were then living, and found a grassy spot beside a quiet inlet from Nickajack Lake. The bream were hitting worms. Big ones, almost the size of my hand. We caught ten of these, plus a small bass. Josh reeled in three himself, squealing with delight every time. His first fish. A pretty good catch for a three-year-old.

I intend to take him and Jessica again. Very soon.

I started thinking: Maybe when I'm older, much older, and a little feeble, Josh or another grown-up grandkid will remember to come and see me. I won't be feeling so well, but he'll say, "C'mon Grandpa, let me take ya fishin'."

I'll go if I have to be carried.

Maybe we'll find a secret place, a hidden den of bass, just waiting to be caught.

TWELVE

That "Good" Ole Mountain Dew

On a cold drizzly afternoon we were glad to see Cousin Lonzo, the nearest thing to Li'l Abner I ever knew. Lonzo had his fiddle and it didn't take much encouragement for him to strike up a familiar tune in our store.

> *Down the road here from me,*
> *There's an old holler tree,*
> *Where you lay down a dollar 'er two.*
> *Then you go around the bend,*
> *And when you come back ag'in,*
> *There's a jug full*
> *Of good ole mountain dew.*

All the men and boys around the potbellied stove were singing and tapping their feet.

Oh, they call it that good ole mountain dew,
   And them that refuse it 're few.
I'll shut up my mug, if ye'll fill up my jug
   With that good ole mountain dew.

"Whoopee!"

"Hit it, Lonzo!"

"Play it, boy!"

Mama was frowning behind the counter. When Lonzo stopped for a breather, she was ready. "Boys, I call it that bad ole mountain dew. Don't any of you think of doing any drinking in here."

" 'Course not, Hester. We wuz jist sangin'. Hain't no harm in that, is thar?"

"I'd better not see you drinking that poison in here."

Mama hated whiskey more than anything else. She let us kids know, and she let Daddy know. Only once did I ever know of him coming home drunk. When he didn't get up the next morning, she went over and pulled the covers from his head. "I've got a tarrible toothache," he moaned.

She smelled his breath. "Where's your whiskey?"

He meekly pulled a fruit jar from under the bed. "Take it outside, James Carl, and break it," she ordered me grimly. "Fred, I'm ashamed of you, comin' home like this and lettin' your kids see you drunk."

Daddy begged forgiveness. So far as I know, he never drank again.

I never took a sip of spirits. Howard Jean admits to a few sips, but he was never drunk. I don't think our sisters ever got near a jug or fruit jar of corn liquor. Mama was the main reason. But we also knew that a lot of what passed for moonshine was half kerosene.

Moonshine was sneaked into our store when Mama wasn't watching. I also saw men slide into Lloyd's feed room and come out with strong breath. They drank in the bushes around brush arbor meetings and behind the school house during pie suppers and other community doings. They passed the fruit jar in Cousin Harry's garage where a poker game ran every Saturday. But they didn't drink before Mama or she would have run them out with a broom.

Most of the drinking in Judy was done on Saturday. When a fellow would pass out, his buddies would drag him into the hollow.

As more men got cars (few women ever drove) drinking became more dangerous. Uncle Loma, the constable, vowed to stop the drinking in Judy.

One Saturday Uncle Loma saw George Hankins' Model A sedan come weaving up the road. He ran out with his pistol and yelled, "Stop!" When George didn't, Uncle Loma peppered the car with pistol bullets. George raced right on through the town and over Graveyard Hill to Dry Branch. He buried ten gallons of raw whiskey in a hideout, then turned around and came back and stopped before Uncle Loma's gun in front of our store.

"You boys stay in here," Mama yelled at me and Howard Jean, but she was too late. We ran into the crowd that was milling around Uncle Loma and George. Big Odell, one overall gallus flapping, was glowerin' at the constable. "You came purt near to killin' my buddy." Uncle Loma wiggled his gun. "Git back!"

"You tellin' me what to do?" the big fellow snarled. "Take that gun off and I'll whip the stuffin' out of ye."

I saw another fellow moving toward Uncle Loma. Uncle Bill ran up and grabbed him. "See, Ole Son, this is none of your business. Loma's the law hyar."

"I'm taking George to jail," Uncle Loma announced.

Daddy stepped up between his brother and George, who was related to Mama by marriage. "No need to take him to jail. I'll go his bail."

Daddy and Uncle Loma argued, but finally Uncle Loma gave in. Tempers cooled and a date was set for George's trial.

Uncle Will Smith, the Freewill Baptist preacher, was then Justice of the Peace. He presided from the big barber chair in our store. He called witnesses, then the jury retired to a long bench out back of the store. I slipped around to hear the jury deliberating. They voted George guilty and Uncle Will assessed a fine.

Making moonshine went with the territory in "dry" Newton County. Prohibition came and went and few knew the difference.

Moonshine was also called wildcat, rotgut, and White Mule. The story goes that Tom Reynolds was hunting squirrels near John Dale's still at a spring on Hinson Creek. Tom stopped off to get a snort and bent over to light his pipe from the fire heating the boiler.

The stopper in his powder horn fell out. The powder fell into the fire, igniting with a bang, and throwing old Tom backwards. He got to his feet, declaring,

"Dale, that White Mule shore kin kick."

Making whiskey was legitimate before Prohibition, so long as the operator was licensed and paid the proper taxes. Mama's grandfather, Dr. Simon Sutton, was authorized to make bonded whiskey. He sold it in the county and shipped to customers outside. Three of his sons reportedly made wildcat.

The repeal of Prohibition brought an economic boom to Newton County. During the 1930s and '40s stave-cutting was the biggest industry in the area. Five mills operated in Newton County alone.

Timber cutters toppled the finest oaks in the woods. Using crosscut saws, they sawed the logs into short lengths, then hammered wedges in the ends to split into stave bolts. Truckload after truckload of oak stave bolts rolled through Judy on the way to the stave mills where the wood was sliced into staves and shipped to distant distilleries for making barrels in which to season whiskey.

Only one man in the valley ever refused to make stave bolts. Uncle Dan Hefley, the Holiness preacher, was working in the timber one day when a fellow said, "Seems mighty strange, ye bein' a preacher and helpin' the devil."

"How's that?" asked Uncle Dan.

"Hain't ye thought about these stave bolts goin' into whiskey barrels?"

"No, I hain't," said the preacher, "but I'm a'thinkin' of it now." He picked up his saw, hat, and wedges and went home.

If Mama made the connection, she never said anything about it. She must have known that every store in town benefited from the stave bolt boom.

Mama was that way with chewing and smoking tobacco and dipping snuff. She hated nicotine in any form and predicted all kinds of dire sicknesses for users. But she said, "If I don't have tobacco on the shelf, people won't come in to buy groceries." We kids knew she had better not catch us sampling any. Daddy didn't tell us not to, but we noticed that he didn't mess with tobacco himself.

After repeal, Newton and surrounding counties voted to stay dry. The nearest legal whiskey was over the Missouri state line. Most drinkers couldn't afford to go that far or didn't have transportation, so they imbibed moonshine.

The moonshiners took a great interest in the sheriff's race. Still it was kind of hard for a sheriff to avoid making arrests, especially with a federal revenuer looking over his shoulder. Eluding the law got to be quite a sport.

Sheriff John Monroe Hallums came upon my Uncle Jobie just as he was about to light a fire under his boiler near a spring. The sheriff looked around and couldn't find any liquor. "W'al, Jobie," he said, " 'pears ye've either sold or hid all y'er wildcat. Jist go ahead and light y'er f'ar and run me off some evidence."

Uncle Jobie rose up like a rooster priming for a fight. "F'ar up the boiler yerself, Sheriff. I ain't makin' no evidence to convict me."

Failing in that strategy, the sheriff made a wider search. This time he found a full five-gallon jug in a bluff crevice.

"I've got ye now, Jobie. C'mon and let's go."

Uncle Jobie became downright agreeable. He offered to be helpful. "Sheriff, that jug is a mou't heavy fer ye to pack. I'll take it a little ways, if ye'd like."

The sheriff looked at Jobie and cracked, "Ye're a smart one, ole boy. Ye'll drap that jug and destroy the evidence. I ain't that big a fool."

Uncle Jobie grinned and kept walking. When they reached the car, Sheriff Hallums reminded him, "Y'er grandpa and I have been friends all our life. Fer his sake, I'll accept y'er promise that ye'll be in Jasper Saturday for trial, and I won't take ye to jail."

Uncle Jobie promised. He was there for the trial and got off with a fine. A man's word, moonshiner or not, was his bond in Newton County.

Cousin Zack, who is on Daddy's side of the family, was reputed to be the biggest moonshiner in the county. Uncle Joey, who is on Mama's side and also made his share, accused Cousin Zack of "making the sorriest whiskey of any of us, but we couldn't beat 'em sellin' hit. Ole Zack could sell a blind feller a lookin' glass."

Uncle Joey had a good line himself for customers: "Take one drank and hit gits lonesome in your belly all by itself. Take anuther'n and hit starts a fight. Then ye hafta take a third 'un for a jedge 'tween the 'tuther two, and take some more fer a jury."

Uncle Joey gulped enough moonshine to float Noah's ark. He can still stand on his feet at seventy-five. "Fellers lak me," he claims, "kin drunk all their lives and never git to be an alcahawlic." He still enjoys a snort or two.

Last time I saw Uncle Jobie and Cousin Zack, both said they had quit.

Declared Uncle Jobie: "The last time I got drunk, I fell all over the place and skinned my face and arms. I seed myself in the lookin' glass and thought, 'Ole Boy, keep this up and ye ain't gonna be long fer this ole world.' I tolt myself, 'This is your last 'un.' I quit. Them boys come by and said, 'Jist take a little sip, it ain't gonna hurt ye.' I answered 'em, 'I know it ain't gonna hurt me, cuz I quit.'

"Not long after that, I turned to the Lord. Repented and asked his forgiveness. Me and my family, we'uns started us a little church right hyar 'side air house. We go thar ever' Sunday."

Cousin Zack told a similar story. "One day I woke up and saw whar that wildcat whiskey wuz a'takin' me. I started thinkin' about whar I wuz goin' to spend eternity. I got down on my knees and asked the Lord to make me a new man. He shore did. Now I'm a'goin' to the Assembly of God church and Sunday school ever' Sunday and a'livin' for the Lord. Hit's a wonderful life."

Sheriff Russell Burdine of Red Rock probably closed down more stills than any lawman in the history of Newton County. I knew Russell very well. He was a close friend of our family. His son William married one of my twin sisters, Loucille.

Russell took an occasional drink himself. In fact, after his term was up, he patronized a moonshiner he once arrested. But while in office, Russell vowed to enforce the law. "The law says hit's illegal to make whiskey in Newton County, and I'm a'gonna arrest anybody I ketch doin' it."

Russell pulled down thirty-nine convictions before hanging up his star after only one term. But he struck out a few times.

He was sure Lem Gurney was making and selling corn liquor. He searched the old man's cabin and premises a half dozen times without finding any evidence. Every time he came around, Lem's old hound barked and snarled as if he wanted the sheriff for breakfast. Consequently, Russell didn't go near the doghouse. After Lem died, Russell went to help the new owner move in. Suddenly it occurred to him where Lem had been hiding his whiskey. Sure enough, there was a secret compartment in the doghouse.

One afternoon Russell and a revenuer walked up on an old bewhiskered fellow sleeping beside a still. Russell shook him awake and told him he was under arrest.

"What fer, Sheriff?" the old man asked in an innocent tone.

"Fer makin' illegal whiskey. The evidence is rat hyar 'side ye."

"W'al shore nuff, thar is some whiskey here, but hit ain't mine. I wuz out huntin' my hawgs and come across this still. Took me a little drink and laid down. Must have dozed off."

Russell took him to court but lost the case.

Every community had its share of rowdies who got drunk and created trouble around pie suppers and church meetings. One of the worst bunch of toughs was at Nail. One evening Russell got word they were intending to break up a revival meeting. His deputy was out of the county, so he deputized his son, sixteen-year-old William. The two drove to the Nail store and parked.

Russell handed his son a gun. "Drive out the road ten miles and turn around and come back. If you see me in the road, stop. If not, keep a'goin'."

William followed instructions. As he rounded the curve coming back to Nail he saw his dad's stocky figure and the star gleaming on his chest. He slammed the car to a halt.

"Open the back door, Son. I've got us some company."

William complied while his dad ran up the hill to a barbwire fence. William heard some commotion and jangling of metal. Then a man in handcuffs came rolling down the hill. "Throw 'em in the car, Son," Russell called. "Anutherin's comin'."

A second came tumbling toward him in the dark. Then a third, fourth, and fifth. All handcuffed with their hands bloodied from the barbwire.

"How'd you git 'em Daddy?" William asked.

"Twarn't no trouble, Son. I jist took 'em one at a time and handcuffed 'em to the fence."

The moonshine making, the altercations, and runins with the law, and the carousing and fighting are not the whole story. Mama knew, we all knew, and we all suffered from moonshine-related tragedies within our circle of kin.

Mama's Uncle Maynard was the best jackleg lawyer Newton County ever produced. He was a skilled engineer and surveyor. He and his close friend Joe Vaughn probably marked off half the land boundaries in the county. Ole Joe was the county mystery man. He came into the community of Boxley in midlife and married a local girl without people knowing who he was. On his deathbed Joe confessed to being Frank

James, brother of the famous outlaw, Jessie James. Two members of his family investigated everything he said and wrote a book to prove that he really was Frank James, although their views are disputed by historians.

Joe Vaughn could not hold a light to Uncle Maynard's drinking. Uncle Maynard might have made it to the governor's mansion if he'd left moonshine alone. I saw him many times in Judy, with his bleary eyes and red nose, as he stumbled along the road. Once he dozed off on a bench on our porch and Daddy mischievously poured some quinine into his mouth. That brought him awake.

Uncle Maynard told ghost stories that would turn your blood to ice. He could take his teeth out, touch his chin to his nose, and contort his face in ways that kept everybody laughing. I loved this old man who was Grandma Barbara's brother. I wanted to cry when I saw him drunk.

Mama had only two brothers. Sad to say, they both drank heavily. Uncle Hardy always felt ill at ease among young people, apparently because of a severe speech impediment. He was only about ten years older than I and one of the kindest and gentlest young men I ever knew. He married a pretty girl from Big Creek and they had three beautiful children. I spent the night with them a number of times. I saw him laughing and romping with his kids.

Uncle Hardy started drinking. Maybe he picked it up from his Uncle Maynard, maybe he didn't think it was wrong because his father, Grandpa Pulliam, took a swig now and then. Maybe he was influenced by other Sutton uncles. Maybe they were influenced by their father, the doctor who made legal whiskey. You can't pin the blame except to say that he was around drinkers as a boy.

Uncle Hardy would come into our store half drunk. Mama would pull him aside. I'd hear them talking. "Hardy, go home to your family and leave that ole whiskey alone," she pleaded. Sometimes she'd say, "Hardy, you're my little brother. I'd give anything, if you'd quit." He'd promise, and then the next time she saw him, he'd have moonshine on his breath.

Uncle Hardy got to where he couldn't make a living on his farm. He and his wife opened a little grocery business in Judy. They didn't have a chance, as there were too many stores in Judy already. His wife then took a job in Harrison, driving back and forth every day. They began having marital problems. Uncle Hardy took to drinking more. She filed for divorce.

The day the divorce became final he called her at her work on the telephone (not long after phones were installed in Judy) and told her he was going to kill himself. She immediately called Jeames Nichols in the cafe across the road from their store. Jeames heard the shotgun blast before he could get there. He found Uncle Hardy lying on the floor, dead.

Uncle Bert, Mama's other brother, also drank and was divorced by his wife, who was Daddy's sister. Their son was one of my favorite cousins. I stayed at their house many nights.

Uncle Bert lived with Grandpa and Grandma Foster until they died. After that, Mama was his mainstay. She'd beg him to leave whiskey alone. He'd promise, then go out and get drunk. Like Uncle Hardy, my Uncle Bert was kind and thoughtful. He just couldn't refuse a drink.

He lived about a quarter mile from Mama and Daddy and took his meals with them. One evening he was late. My baby sister Patsy was then in high school and Mama sent her down to call him.

"Uncle Bert, come to supper," she called from outside. When there was no answer, she pushed open the door and looked inside. There he lay on the floor, blood covering his face and neck. Patsy was terrified. She ran out, screaming, "Get an ambulance! Uncle Bert has killed himself."

They got him to the hospital in Harrison where the doctors saved his life.

Uncle Bert checked into the nursing home in Harrison. Whiskey wasn't available there. He developed a friendship with a fine woman and married her in the home. They had a few happy months together before he died from a fatal heart attack at sixty-five.

Drinking wasn't as bad on Daddy's side of the family as on Mama's. Yet there are a couple of stories I must tell.

Cousin Lonzo was a big, broad-shouldered, good-looking man, strong as an ox, with a dark curly lock twirling over his forehead that made the girls' hearts flutter. He could shake a persimmon tree that I couldn't move and down would come Mr. 'Possum. He would sit on the creek bank all night, laughing and telling stories, having a good time, even when the fish weren't biting. When two of us began scuffling, he would say, "No need to git so riled up." Then if we didn't stop, he would reach out with a giant paw and pull us apart.

He may have been a little dense. Sometimes he was incredibly naive and would believe anything you told him. He was too shy to look straight at a girl. But when he put his bow to a fiddle, you knew you were hearing talent.

Everybody teased Cousin Lonzo. You could tickle him, scare him, but you couldn't make him mad.

Lonzo was deathly afraid of ghosts. He lived on the mountain above the head of Big Creek. A walk to Judy from there took all day and part of the evening. He'd stop and spend the night at the Bryants' to keep from having to pass the Sexton cemetery in the dark.

One night R.L. and Conrad Bryant took him hunting. The brothers carried guns and Lonzo packed an ax to chop a coon out of a hole. They led him behind a neighbor's house where the wife had left white sheets hanging out overnight.

Conrad ran ahead in the darkness, ducked behind the clothesline, and fluffed a sheet at Lonzo. "Lordy, a ghost!" Lonzo screamed. He ran at the sheet and split it wide open with his ax. If Conrad hadn't been back a couple of feet, Lonzo might have killed him.

The Bryant brothers and their neighbor, Arnold Holt, set up another scare. R.L. took Lonzo along a trail skirting the top of a bluff. Suddenly Conrad, wrapped in a sheet, raised up in the middle of the trail before them. Lonzo turned and ran back along the trail in fright. He came around a tree and met another sheet-bedecked figure—Arnold.

Right behind Lonzo and pretending to be scared, R.L. started up a small tree. Lonzo pulled him back.

"Not that little 'un, R.L. Climb one we kin both git up."

We all loved to play tricks on Lonzo. One night we were fishing a deep hole on Piney Creek for catfish. Monk slipped up the bank and swam back downstream underwater until he picked up Lonzo's bait. Then he swam out with it.

Lonzo's reel screamed. "Boys, I've got me the biggest yeller-bellied cat in the creek!" Monk "played" Lonzo skillfully, swimming out, turning, splashing, blowing spray, diving under, finally leaping above the water, pulling the line and letting the bait fly back in Lonzo's face.

"Dadnab it!" Lonzo exclaimed in disgust. "Dadnab it to the devil, boys. I let that ole yeller-belly git away." Our sides were heaving. I ran off in the darkness to keep Lonzo from hearing me laugh.

"Dadnab it, boys, I'm a'comin' back next Saturday and set hyar all night to catch that ole yeller-belly."

Nobody ever told Lonzo that the "yeller-belly" catfish was only his cousin Monk.

Lonzo took only an occasional drink at first, as most teenage boys did. Then he began fiddling for square dances and discovered that he didn't feel shy after one or two swallows. "C'mon, Lonz, have another 'un," they would say. He just couldn't say no.

His parents saw what was happening. They pleaded to no avail. He'd stay sober a couple of days, then a couple of guys would come by and coax him to play for their next jamboree. Once there, he'd take a drink to loosen up and be gone again.

Twice he entered the National Fiddling contest at Mt. Sherman, Arkansas. The second time he advanced to the finals and probably would have won if he hadn't been half tight while playing.

His real friends would tell him, "Lonz, you're killin' yerself." He'd say, "I know it, boys, and I'm a tryin' to quit, but they jist won't leave me alone."

His drunks got longer, his sober periods shorter. He had to have the booze now.

His family took him to Little Rock for treatment. He died in a hospital there; the technical cause, according to the medical report, was kidney poisoning. He was twenty-nine years old.

The funeral director took one look at my cousin Lonzo, still a strapping hulk of a man, with his L'il Abner locks curling over a smooth forehead. "What in the world killed such a handsome young man?" the mortician asked. Everybody knew it was moonshine.

Cousin Tom Jack was a different story, but the end was the same. One afternoon we were playing basketball on the dirt court in front of Judy School. He happened to have a car. The next day he and a friend picked up a couple of girls and went to the state line for licensed booze. On the way back they rounded Bear Creek Curve north of Harrison at high speed and hit a traveling salesman head on. Tom Jack and the salesman were killed, the others critically injured.

Last year I went back to the county for the wedding ceremony of my nephew, Boyce D. Burdine. Boyce is my sister Loucille's son and the grandson of the late Sheriff Burdine. Boyce was marrying lovely Carolyn Carney from Nail. Her father was there to give her away. Her mother couldn't make the wedding. She and her sister had been killed by a seventy-one-year-old drunk driver traveling on the wrong side of the road.

People are finally getting fed up with the abuse of alcohol. It's been a long time coming, and about time, too. Some who have lost loved ones are joining organizations such as RID (Remove Intoxicated Drivers) and MADD (Mothers Against Drunk Drivers).

Mama was definitely RID and 100 percent MADD forty years ago. And not just about drunk drivers.

The world is just catching up to Mama.

She knew that song about "good ole mountain dew" was a lie.

THIRTEEN
The Old Timers

Saturday started in Judy when Cousin Lloyd sauntered slowly past our porch on his way to the post
office.

Then came Uncle Pete Collins, walking in from his
mountain cabin. Uncle Pete, around ninety, part
Choctaw Indian, sported an enormous walrus moustache. He was heard to boast that he had never taken
a bath in his life.

Monk and I were on our porch looking to see what
we could see. "H'air ye, Uncle Pete?" Monk called.

Uncle Pete turned sourly toward us, shifted the
cud of tobacco from one leathery jaw to another, and
grumped, "How'd ye lack to be called, 'Hairy Uncle
Pete'?" Then, without further word, he marched on
to the post office to check his mail. Monk or I ad-
dressed him that way every Saturday morning and
he always replied the same.

If it was a cold day, the men gathered around the
potbellied stove in our store. If warm, they lounged

on the porches, swapping yarns, exchanging twists of homegrown chewing tobacco, spitting at hound dogs, and telling President Roosevelt how he should run the country and the war effort.

We didn't see that many women. When a woman did come into our store, she usually didn't hang around long. Men generally bought the groceries. Mama always asked about their women folks.

"She's home cannin'," they'd say. "Workin' in her garden." "Takin' care of a sick young'un." Or, "She's feelin' poorly today."

"Well, why don't you bring her next time?"

"I'll see if she kin come, Hester."

Whittling was more of a problem than spitting. Mama kept a pan in front of the stove for a cuspidor. Outside, they could always spit off the porch. But when they didn't bring along a piece of wood, they whittled on the benches and even on the four-by-fours which held up our porch roof. Daddy saw that the galvanized iron roof would fall unless preventive action was taken. We hammered metal strips around the supports. That saved our porch.

We boys didn't play horseshoes or marbles or fish or hunt all the time outside of school. We spent many hours leaning against a bench or stretched out on the porch, listening to the lore of the elders.

Uncle Willie Pink was my favorite storyteller. By the time we were living in the back of the store, he was running a blacksmith shop beyond Nichols' Cafe and was too busy for entertaining. Next to Uncle Willie, I liked Alfred Smith, a stocky little man who was descended from the famous feuding Smiths.

Alfred had been a timber hauler in his younger days. "Boys, I wuz a'comin' down Silent Mountain with a load of lumber on my old Dodge," he told us one morning. "My brakes give out on the grade and I couldn't git it in low. I wuz goin' ninety mile an air when I seed this cow at the bottom of the last hill. Smack dab in the middle of the road she wuz."

He always paused so we could appreciate the gravity of the situation.

"Boys, I couldn't gear 'er down 'er stop. I did the only thang left. I poured on the gay-us and jumped that ole cow as clean as a whistle."

He paused again.

"When I hit the ground I was goin' so fast that I coasted up the other mountain."

Alfred also had a legendary Dodge sedan. One day when the creek was too high for the mail truck to cross, he remarked, "Ole Noil [the mail man], he don't know how to cross a creek. I don't go in at the ford whar' the water is swift. No, siree. I go up to the bank of the deep hole, gun the motor, and take a run at it. That ole Dodge is a'goin' so fast, hit walks on water."

The best thing about Alfred was that he told his stories as if they had really happened. Then he stood up and said, "Boys, I've best be gettin' home." He knew when to leave for the right effect.

Many stories pointed up the genius of Big Creek "boys" in outwitting or making "smart" remarks to outsiders. The classics were told so many times about so many different "boys" it is impossible to recall the original author. Examples:

"Thar was this ole boy who went to see his uncle in Muskogee, Oklahomee. People would come by and show 'em a dime and a nickel and tell 'em, 'Take yer pick.' He'd allus grab the nickel and they'd hoo-raw about how dumb them Arkansawyers air. They must've done that to 'em a thousand times, when one day a feller pulled him aside and 'splained the difference. The ole boy said, 'Shucks, I knowed that 'fore I come hyar.' 'W'al, why do ye keep takin' the nickel?' 'Cuz, if I'se ever to take the dime, them dern fools would never try me agin.'"

"This ole boy was fishin' down by the Lyles' Bluff when the game warden come by and seed he had an eight-inch bass on his stringer. 'That 'uns two inches too little,' the game warden said. 'Reckon I'll hafta take ye in.'

"'Oh, but I warn't plannin on takin' hit home,' the old boy tolt 'em.

"The game warden decided he'd play along with 'em. 'Jist what w'ar ye plannin' on doin' with that little 'un?'"

"'Tarn hit loose before I go home. Hit's been botherin' me all day. I'd ketch hit and tarn hit loose. Then I'd ketch hit agin and tarn hit loose. Ever' time I'd tarn hit loose, hit'd come right back and take my bait agin. Atter while I thought I'd tie hit up and give the big 'uns a chance."

All else stopped when a stranger came into Judy. We looked to bespectacled Uncle Bill Hefley to get the information we wanted.

His interrogation ran like this:

"See, ole son, don't I know ye from somewhar?"

"No, sir, I don't recall ever meeting you."

"W'al, you kinda look lack an Ederdge [Edwards]."

"No, that isn't my name."

"You wouldn't be kin to any of the Greenhaws would ye?"

"No, sir."

"What did ye say yer name wuz?"

"I didn't."

"W'al, I shore thought ye wuz an Ederdge or a Greenhaw."

"I'm a Campbell."

"W'al, then would you happen to be kin to Elmer Camel's [Campbell] bunch?"

"No, sir. I don't know that I have any relatives in this community."

"You're jist passin' through?"

"No, I came here to see a Mr. Lloyd Hefley."

"That's my son. That's his place of bizness, right thar. I'll take ye in and introduce ye. 'Er, what'd ye say yer bizness wuz?"

"I didn't."

"W'al, ye wouldn't be a post office 'specter by any chance?"

"I might."

"Come on, I'll take ye in. My son will be proud to see ye. Keeps ever'thang in good order. We don't trifle with Uncle Sam. No, sir, we respect the federal government. We're proud ye come to visit us."

One morning a well-dressed lady stopped. Uncle Bill put her through the usual grilling. Finally she blushed and said, "All I wanted was to use a rest room. Would you happen to have one in there?"

Uncle Bill smiled over his spectacles. "Oh, shore, sister. Jist go in and rest all ye want. Thar's cold pop in the icebox."

Uncle Bill was a little younger than my Grandpa Tom. While his brother tended to hunting and bee-keeping, Uncle Bill put his stock in education. He talked the dialect, but he was easily the most worldly-wise man in Judy. In his prime he was six foot four and a bit of a dandy. On a hot summer day you'd see him walking to Judy, straight as a hickory sapling, sporting a clean, stiff white shirt and creased pants, and shading himself with a flower parasol. For this and his height he was called "High Bill."

Three of his sons became school teachers; a fourth, Lloyd, had the post office and a general store for over forty years; while a fifth, Kenneth, operated a garage.

Uncle Bill was always the man to see about school business. He was a fixture on the board and the man whose approval you needed if you were to teach. To his credit, he finally realized that if the school were to advance, outside help would have to be sought.

One day a tall, angular stranger drove up. Uncle Bill pried and probed, making no headway. Finally he stated forthwith: "Ole son, what is yer bizness with us?"

The visitor looked him in the eye and snorted, "None of yers, ole man!"

He walked stiffly into the store and was sent right back to Uncle Bill. He was the new candidate for school superintendent. Uncle Bill voted to hire him, "'Cuz we need a feller who won't put up with any foolishness."

Uncle Bill was a widower and in his sixties before we moved to Judy. All the eligible widows had their eyes on him. But he played the field, keeping his eyes out for a young woman.

Uncle Joe, his younger brother—the one we knew as Cross-eyed Joe—and also a widower, remarried. On a visit to Judy from Oklahoma, he plainly told Uncle Bill, "You ain't a sprang chicken anymore. Don't jist be lookin' for them young'uns."

Uncle Bill kept looking. Once a week he caught a ride to Harrison. He'd walk around the courthouse awhile, then set up headquarters at Val Bennett's drugstore. Val knew him, as everybody did, and had a special chair reserved for him. "See, ole son, I'm gonna set hyar and rest," Uncle Bill told Val. "When a young womern comes in that you think I oughta meet, introduce me. Jist don't waste my time with any over forty."

Uncle Bill belonged to the Judy Church of Christ, as did most all of Grandpa Jim Hefley's descendants. He was a respected elder and Sunday school teacher, the man the visiting preachers took dinner with.

In this regard, he was the local Bible scholar and could quote whole chapters by memory. Saturday mornings he came early to Judy, eager to "contend for the faith" as he saw it.

Uncle Bill's principal adversaries were Riley Sexton, a farmer from Dry Creek with arms like Paul Bunyan, and Uncle Dan Hefley, the loose-jointed Pentecostal preacher, who seemed to go on forever. They provided the fireworks every Saturday, as they sat on the post office porch and hurled verses at each other from their big King James Bibles. If there wasn't an interesting dogfight or horseshoe game going, or if Alfred wasn't spinning a yarn, this trio had a pretty good audience.

Riley was the younger of the three and probably the smartest. He had a smile that could melt icicles off a bluff, and a hearty laugh that you could hear all the way to Uncle Willie Pink's blacksmith shop. He was married to Mama's first cousin, Bonnie Nichols. They lived in a rustic log cabin above Dry Creek, beside the trail that led to Grandpa Pulliam's place. On our way to Honey Creek we often saw him working in his cornfield, plowing and cussing his mules, or if the weather was bad, he'd be sitting on his porch reading the Bible.

Riley professed no faith. He could cuss and exhale Scripture in the same breath. He usually took Uncle Dan's side, since Uncle Bill was smarter than the preacher.

When Riley got Uncle Bill trapped—as few people ever did—he'd slap his knee, spit a stream of tobacco juice at an old dog, and laugh like he'd struck a gold mine. But he also liked to see Uncle Dan squirm—and anyone else who had a deep faith.

Uncle Dan knew his way around in the Good Book. He could recite the commandments and the Sermon on the Mount forwards and backwards. But there were times when Riley and Uncle Bill could tie him in knots. In his approach to religion, Riley was my kind of man. I figured one church was as good as another and there was no need for me to tie in with either the Church of Christ or the Holiness.

Some folks were critical of visiting preachers. They'd come into Judy wearing suit coats and neckties, visit around the community, eat chicken dinners, give a talk every night for a week at the school house, and take away a hundred dollars. "That thar's mighty good pay for jist talkin' about the Bible," Riley said. "I do it fer nuthin'."

I listened to Riley with an admiring ear. I respected Uncle Bill and thought he was right smart in ways. If that was his religion, and it made him happy, fine. Live and let live.

Uncle Dan was more of a bother. He could act so terribly corny and backwoodsy, yet he was such a good and happy man. He pulled teeth, sat up with the sick, walked twenty miles to preach a funeral, and never charged a penny. No one had ever heard of him taking up a collection and he had been preaching two and three times a week for forty years. And no one ever saw him when he didn't have a smile on his face.

Stories about him were legend. Before he got a Model A, he rode an old deaf mule named Jude to meetings. People would hear him coming back up Big Creek on Sunday night after his meeting, singing and praying, bringing the names of neighbors before the Lord.

One night at a meeting he tied up Ole Jude. As he was walking away, the mule let him have it right in the rear. Only the New Testament in his back pocket kept him from getting hurt. All he said was, "Thank the Lord."

Another night he arrived early for meeting and walked up a little hollow to pray. Two men rode up behind him and one pushed a gun barrel under his nose. "Ye're gonna stop this prayin' and preachin' and git out of air community," he said.

Uncle Dan stared right back. "Son, if'n you pull that trigger, before the sound leaves this holler I'll be in heaven."

The fellow put away his gun and they rode off without saying another word.

Uncle Dan had seven grown children. They all went to meetings with him. His son Berry was asked, "What does your daddy say when he hits his finger with a hammer?"

" 'Count it all joy.' I've heard him say that a thousand times."

Berry said his daddy had a long bench in their front room, set apart for a home altar. "Morning, dinnertime, and night, Daddy calls us thar to pray. We git down on air knees an' talk to the Lord."

You could hear the shouting and singing a mile before you got to one of Uncle Dan's meetings. He held one every August, after the crops were laid by, near where Dry Creek runs into Big Creek. We Judy boys would go and watch from the treetops.

They cleared a quarter acre in the woods, covered the ground with sawdust, and snaked in logs for benches. Lanterns were hung on tree limbs to give light, and babies laid on pallets beside the logs.

By the time we arrived and shinnied up the trees, Uncle Dan's long-limbed daughters were playing guitars and singing, and the preacher was clapping his hands to warm up the crowd.

> *Praise the Lord!*
> *When a man is born of God,*
> *He is washed in Jesus' blood.*

> *He goes in for doin' good,*
> *Praise the Lord!*
>
> *Praise the Lord!*
> *He's got a second birth.*
> *He is filled with holy mirth!*
> *He's the happiest man on earth,*
> *Praise the Lord.*

Uncle Dan was up and dancing around the benches, being careful not to step on any babies. "Glory! Glory! Glory! I feel happy tonight, folks. Hallelujah! I've got the joy of the Lord in my bones. Whooooooie! Ain't it wunnerful! Whooooie! Glory to God!"

His wife and children started hollering. Others joined them. Round and round they went, kicking sawdust, shouting, and singing. Having a rip-roaring good time.

After awhile Uncle Dan got them to sit down. He kicked off the testifying with his own experience.

"Back when I was a boy, praise the Lord, I got under conviction. Yes, under conviction. Hallelujah! I couldn't sleep. The Holy Ghost kept a bringin' up my sins 'fore me. Amen! Glory to God. I went to that ole-time altar. I tolt the Lord, 'I'm gonna be hyar all night on ma knees, till I git saved. All night, Lord. Hallelujah!' I prayed, and I prayed. I called on the Lord. The Bible says, 'Who-so-ever shall call on the name of the Lord shall be saved.' Not mou't 'er maybe, but 'shall be saved.' I called on the Lord, and, glory to God, he saved me. He set me free, yes, he set me free. Hallelujah, glory to God, he broke the bonds of prison for me. Well, ha, ha, ha,

I tell ye folks, I couldn't sleep that night 'cuz I wuz so a'happy. Glory to God! Ain't hit wunnerful! Anybody else wanna testify? Come right on up! Hallelujah!"

The testifying went on for an hour. Then Uncle Dan preached an hour. He told about "gittin' the Holy Ghost." He said, "I was saved but I couldn't understan' what people meant by gittin' the Holy Ghost. Amen. Glory to God. I desired that 'sperience. I wanted it. I sought the Lord. Hallelujah, yes, I sought the Lord. One night I was up preaching in a school house. Hallelujah! I felt the power of the Holy Ghost come on me. Glory to God! I was floatin' 'tween the ceiling and the floor. Amen! Amen! Amen! I was havin' me a time. I got the Holy Ghost. Glory to God! Ye kin get the Spirit too. Tonight, God wants to bless ye."

He preached to sinners awhile, then his family struck up a song that raised chill bumps on my neck. It was a sort of dialogue between a man and Death.

> *What is this that I can see?*
>   *Cold icy hands takin' hold of me.*
> *I am Death none can expel.*
>   *There is a heaven, there is a hell!*
>   *I'll fix y'er feet so ye cain't walk.*
>   *I'll lock y'er jaws so ye cain't talk.*
> *I'll close yer eyes so ye cain't see.*
>   *This very 'air ye must go with me.*

The song ran on and on, the sinner pleading with Death to leave him alone, to give him more time. Finally, Death's last word,

> *Too late, too late*
>   *To all farewell.*
> *The doom is fixed.*
>   *The sentence is hell!*

Uncle Dan pleaded for sinners to call on the Lord for mercy. The guitars picked up the familiar altar call and the singers joined in.

> *O why, O why not tonight?*
>   *O why not tonight?*
> *Wilt thou be saved,*
>   *O why not tonight.*

From my perch in a tree I saw the seekers coming to the big log at front, kneeling in the sawdust, and crying for the Lord to save them. Uncle Dan and his family were all around, hugging, kneeling beside mourners, quoting Scripture in their ears, now and then rising up with a happy soul who had "prayed through" and shouting, "Glory to God, another sinner has come home."

The biggest crowds I ever saw in Judy came to a week's revival meeting held by Uncle Dan on the vacant lot beside our store. On a Friday night, I counted a hundred and sixty-seven cars and trucks parked up and down the road. People came from as far north as Harrison and as far south as Russellville.

I saw Uncle Bill off to the side observing and frowning as Uncle Dan and his folks whooped and hollered. This was "foot-warshin'" night, Uncle Dan announced. Several men trotted out a big table on which they placed a large pan of water. Doggone, if

Uncle Dan didn't shuck his shoes and socks and hop up on the table to explain the rite. Uncle Dan never could talk long without dancing. Somebody hollered, "Lookee, Uncle Dan's gonna jump in the pan!"

Sure enough, up he sailed and down he came, both big feet knocking water all around. "Glory to God!" he shouted. "Somebody brang us anuther bucket of water."

Uncle Bill stood by shaking his head in disapproval.

I looked on and wondered, trying to puzzle it all out.

Saturday morning, Uncle Bill wetted his lips when he saw Uncle Dan coming. "Come and let's reason together, Dan," he invited. Uncle Dan didn't need a second invitation. They had hardly started when Riley arrived. A crowd gathered around them.

They debated baptism. Uncle Bill said it was essential to salvation. Uncle Dan believed in "dippin'" the saved all the way under, but "you shore don't have to git baptized to be saved."

Uncle Bill quoted Acts 2:38, "Repent and be baptized . . . for the remission of sins." "Hit's as plain as the nose on yer face, boys. Now why cain't ye believe hit?"

"Hit's symbolic, Bill, that's all," Riley declared. "Cold creek water don't warsh away nobody's sins. If a man has to be baptized to be saved, what air ye gonna do with the thief on the cross who called on the Lord? The Lord tolt 'em, 'Today, ye will be with me in the kingdom.'"

They moved on to miracles. Uncle Bill declared the Lord had rung down the curtain on miraculous healings at the end of the apostolic age. "No, Bill,"

Uncle Dan said, "the Lord is still in the meeracul workin' bizness."

"Maybe he is," Riley countered, "but I ain't seed too many lately."

They disagreed about foot washing. Uncle Bill insisted this was not an ordinance of the church. Uncle Dan declared, "We air duty bound to warsh one another's feet in the worship sarvice."

Uncle Bill got around to the gymnastics in Dan's meetings. "Now, boys, ye know the Bible don't favor people dancing and jumping over benches in worship."

Riley, with a sly grin, handed Uncle Bill his Bible. "Bill, will ye read us Second Samuel, chapter six, and the fourteenth verse."

"Ye're tryin' to trap me, ole son. I know whut it says: 'David danced before the Lord.' Dan's showed me that before. Ye fergit, ole son, that was under the Ole Covenant. There's nuthin' in the New Testament that tells us to dance and jump around in church like a frog."

"Ah, Bill," Dan broke in, "if ye got the Holy Ghost, ye wouldn't talk like that."

"Whut do ye mean, 'git the Holy Ghost'? Enlighten me, ole son."

"Bill, Paul writ in his first letter to the Corinthians, chapter two and verse fourteen, that the natural man receives not the thangs of the Spirit 'cuz they air foolishness to him, neither kin he know them, 'cuz th'ar spiritchally descerned."

The warm June sun had climbed into a blue sky. A horseshoe game drew me away. I returned at noon and Uncle Dan was unfolding his long legs. "I'll pray for ye, boys," he said to Uncle Bill and Riley. "Hit's time I wuz gittin' on home to take care of my stock in time to come back to meetin.'"

Riley also had business elsewhere. The Bible discussion was over for another Saturday.

Sunday morning dawned drowsy and warm. Uncle Bill, as usual, walked down from his son Kenneth's, with whom he was then living. He had his Bible in hand, hoping for another discussion. He took a seat on the porch of the cafe, but nobody wanted to debate him. About nine-thirty, as usual, he peered at his pocket watch. "W'al, boys, hit's 'bout time to be goin' up to Sunday school. Any of ye goin' with me?"

Daddy was at a coon dog field trial. Mama was sewing for the twins. I walked up to David Criner's to see if he wanted to go fishing. Sunday school wasn't on my agenda.

It was on another Sunday morning, long after I left Judy, that Uncle Bill sat on the same porch talking about the Bible. He looked at his watch and said, "W'al, boys, hit's 'bout time to be goin' up to Sunday school." He reached for his Bible and fell to the floor, dead.

Riley Sexton moved to Kansas City. In 1969 he had a heart attack. From his half coma he heard the doctor tell Bonnie, "Your man likely won't make it." In desperation, Riley prayed and became a believer.

I saw Riley several years later, after he had become an Assemblies of God preacher. "I always thought I could handle anythang that come up," he said. "Then I got on my deathbed and had to ask the Lord to take over."

After Riley's death, I stopped by to visit with Bonnie. "Riley and I went down to the barn one evening," she recalled. "He put up an ole sow that was about to have pigs. Then he looked at me and said, 'I'm a gettin' real dizzy.' I turned a five-gallon milk can upside down for him to sit on. He leaned up against the fence, and died."

Uncle Dan preached into his eighties. "It wasn't long after Mama died that he became seriously ill," his daughter Lily remembered. "We took him to the hospital in Harrison, the first time he'd ever been in one in his life. The doctors started building him up for surgery. But the Lord had a different plan. One morning he began quoting the Twenty-third Psalm, 'The Lord is my Shepherd, I shall not want. . . .' He stopped and started again. When he stopped the second time, we called the doctor. By the time he got there, Daddy was with the Lord."

Lily said her nephew, Jim Hefley, had written a song in memory of his grandfather. She played a tape by a singing group composed of his children and grandchildren.

> *Grandpa was an ole time preacher man.*
> *He preached the Word of God throughout the land*
> *He preached so plain a child could understand.*
> *Grandpa was an old time preacher man . . .*

Uncle Dan is buried in a mountain graveyard about twelve miles south of Judy. Uncle Bill is in the burying place on the hill just above Judy. His son Lloyd rests close by. Riley's earthly remains lie beneath the sod in the Sexton cemetery, just across Big Creek from Judy. Most all of the old timers so familiar in my boyhood memories are gone. The Bible men. The tale spinners. The old fellows who whittled and spit and reminisced about their childhood, as I now reminisce about mine.

I stroll through the graveyards and hear the wind whistle in the trees. I see the names on the stones. I remember their faces. I hear their voices.

"How'd ye lack to be called, 'Hairy, Uncle Pete'?"

"I poured on the gay-us and jumped that ole cow clean as a whistle."

"See, ole son, don't I know ye from somewhar?"

"Hit's symbolic, Bill, that's all hit is."

"Glory! Glory! Glory! I feel happy tonight, folks. Hallelujah!"

I drive back to Judy, taking the road I once walked. Johnson's mill is gone, the ground plowed over. The boardwalk before Cousin Lloyd's store porch is falling in. A widow lady now runs the post office in a house up the road not much larger than an outhouse.

Jones' store is crumbling. A new grocery stands where our store was.

A pay telephone stands by the side of the road, just past Lloyd's old store. The top looks like half of an eggshell and totally incongruous in Judy. I punch out my first telephone call from my hometown.

Nichols' Cafe is still operating. I drop in to visit with Jeames and Gussie. They talk about their grandchildren, Junior's kids. We share a story about Junior, Monk's old buddy. Junior lies in the graveyard on the hill. He died of a brain tumor at forty-three.

It is December and cold. Several good ole boys of my generation warm themselves by the stove in the cafe. They talk about what they saw on cable TV last night.

"One generation passes away, and another generation comes" (Ecclesiastes 1:4).

FOURTEEN
Growing Pains

I was the first of over sixty first cousins to graduate from high school and the first to go to college.

Only C. B. Hudson, Junior Johnson, and I were going to Arkansas Tech from our senior class of nine. David Criner was too shy to leave home. Calvin Hill, the fifth boy, had been drafted earlier in the year and would die on Normandy Beach. The four girls—Billie, Dale, Lois, and Jewell—were not interested.

Mama packed my brown tweed $8.98 Sears & Roebuck graduation suit and the remainder of my clothes in a cardboard box. She escorted the girls to a neighbor—Monk had already gone fishing—and Daddy locked up the store.

Daddy lifted my bike over the tailgate of his Model-T truck. I bent to give Ole Shep one last hug and jumped in beside Mama, eager for the great adventure. We were off to Arkansas Tech in Russellville, sixty-five miles away, where I had already mailed my school record.

Daddy was unusually quiet. Mama, I noticed, kept biting her lips. Once I saw her chin quivering.

They drove a mile past the college to George and Jane Essex's house on the outskirts of town. I was to board with them and ride my bike to college. Jane was Mama's cousin and they figured I could be trusted to kinfolks.

Mama took a long time getting ready to go. Daddy kept looking off as if he didn't want us to see his face. Finally he said, "Hester, we'd better git on the road."

"Take good care of the boy," he told George and Jane.

Mama was bawling her head off. She reached out her arms and pulled me to her. "You're so young, James Carl, I don't know if I can stand having you so far away from home."

I tried to be brave. "Aw, I'll be OK, Mama."

"I know you will, but it's still awful hard." She wiped her eyes with the tail of an old sweater she was wearing.

"You be careful on that bicycle and stay out of the way of cars. Study your lessons and get to bed early every night. And Jane, see that he combs his hair and washes his face before leaving for school."

"Come on, Hester," Daddy called.

Mama turned and stepped into the truck. Forty years later she would say that leaving her firstborn in Russellville was the hardest thing she ever did in her life.

The next morning I sped to the campus, parked my bike, and bounced up the stairs to the admission's office in the big white-columned administration building. "Oh, we've been waiting for you," the woman behind the desk gushed. I signed up for a major in business, enrolling in English composition, physical education, Arkansas history, and typing.

A tall, thin blonde tapped my bony shoulder. "I'm a reporter for the *Arka-Tech*." Boy, did I feel important! The story about Tech's youngest student ran in two columns on the front page of the college paper. They gave my age, thirteen; my height, five-seven; weight, one hundred and fifteen pounds; and said I liked Washington Irving, Longfellow, Bret Harte, and Jitters. The last, a comic, ran in the *Arkansas Gazette*. I had seen it for the first time that morning at the Essex's house.

The tweed coat scratched my neck. As soon as I paid my fees, I raced back to my boarding house and jumped into my overalls. By then the neighborhood kids were home from school. I played marbles with a couple of twelve-year-olds. Then we went craw-dadding in a little branch nearby.

The next morning I shuffled bashfully into my first class, wearing overalls. My teachers were all cordial except the supercilious, effeminate-looking dandy who taught English. He no sooner called the roll than he cut me down. "Mr. Hefley, I overheard you tell a classmate, 'I'm not going to no dance tonight.' That is a double negative and will not be tolerated in my class."

I wanted to crawl under the door. I'd never heard of a double negative.

"I assume you passed high school English?"

"Yeah," I mumbled. I knew it wouldn't do any good to tell him that almost everyone at Mount Judy School talked the way I did.

"You're in college now, young man," he continued. "You shall learn to talk and write *proper* English." He bore down on me with an icy stare. "Or, you won't pass *my* course."

I passed every course, except his. I then skipped the summer quarter and went home to catch up on the fishing.

Ole Shep wagged his tail and slobbered all over me. Monk had our reels oiled and was eager to try our luck on Richland.

Mama looked funny when she saw me nuzzling my dog. "James Carl, we had to sell Ole Shep."

"You what?" I couldn't believe it.

"A man came by and offered us twenty dollars. With your college bills and all, we needed the money and. . . ."

"Mama! You didn't!" The enormity of the disaster rolled over me. Shep was only four, and I had counted on having him the rest of my youth.

"Son, there was nobody hyar to take care of 'em," Daddy broke in. "We wuz a'feart he'd run out in the road and git hit by a car."

"The man's already paid you the money?"

"Yup, and he's comin' fer the dog Saturday. We put him off 'til then 'cuz we thought you might want to tell yer dog good-bye."

I intended to do more than say good-bye. Saturday morning, before the sun was up, Ole Shep and I galloped for the creek. I tied him up behind a thick cedar where he wouldn't be seen. About midmorning Daddy and a stranger walked up. They had tracked me down.

"The man wants his dawg, Son," he said sorrowfully.

"He's mine!" I yelled.

"I paid the money for 'em a week ago," the stranger declared.

"Son, whar is he?"

"Daddy, he run off," I lied.

"Woof, woof."

Daddy nodded at the man. He walked behind the cedar and untied *my* dog. I stood there with tears streaming down my face as he led Ole Shep away. Shep kept whining and looking back at me with pleading brown eyes.

"Air ye comin' home with me to eat, Son?"

"No," I sobbed. "I ain't never comin' home."

By night I was cried out. There was also a gnawing in my stomach. But I was a long time forgiving my parents for selling my dog.

I returned to Tech in the fall and moved into the sprawling brick dorm. Having passed my fourteenth birthday, I figured I was quite grown up. Dorm life turned out to be disappointing, however. My assigned roommate, Jo Jo Jones, was a record freak and kept a jam session going twenty hours a day. Now if he had spun Grand Ole Opry discs, I could have stayed in the room. Instead, I fled to the lounge to study.

I was there one evening still trying to figure out double negatives and past perfects for the English course I was repeating, when shouts of "Blackjack!" echoed from a far corner. I strolled over to watch the game and got interested.

They were playing for only a nickel a hand. I watched until I caught on, then I said, "Deal me in," trying to sound professional.

It's a simple game. The dealer gives each player a card face down. You bet that this card plus one or more will beat the dealer's hand. An ace counts one or eleven; a king, queen, or jack, ten; and all other cards are counted at face value. An ace and a picture card make a perfect score. Over twenty-one, and you lose.

I loved Blackjack! I won over a dollar that night, hitting Blackjack six or eight times. "You lucky dog!" an older red-haired boy from Little Rock exclaimed. "You're a real blackjack!"

I played every night. The name stuck. I'd go through the serving line and the girls would say, "What'll it be, Blackjack, beans or cabbage?"

Tech did not have fraternities or sororities. I was eligible for the Business Administration Club, but they expected boys to wear ties to meetings. The agris and engineers acted more my age, but my major ruled me out of both, so I had to watch from the sidelines.

They were having initiations. One morning I came out of the dorm and saw a dozen agri pledges yelling on the sidewalk, "I'm a fool!" An engineer "fish" squatted nearby emptying a bucket of water into another bucket with a thimble. A bunch of his cohorts had been sent to count the bars in the county jail.

All day long they shouted epithets and epigrams around the campus:

"Didja hear about the little agri who thought a mushroom was a place to neck?"

"Do ya know about the little agri who called his girl postscript because her name was Adaline?"

"Didja see the little engineer who slept on his stomach because he heard the Japs were looking for a naval base?"

My kind of guys! Real college material!

Dancing was the most popular social activity, but with so many boys away in the service, the pickings were slim for the girls. There was one flirty little brunette named Marie, who thought I was "so cute." One sunny afternoon after world history class she sweet-talked me into taking her to the dance the following Saturday evening. She didn't ask if I had ever danced before. I could have spared her some pain.

I picked Marie up at Caraway Hall in my $8.98 tweed. She wore a satiny, shimmering blue evening gown. A real knockout if I had been three years older. We made a grand entrance in the streamer-bedecked hall of the Armory. Marie had her arm tucked behind my skinny left elbow and she was smiling as if she had caught a prize mink.

Some of the guys started whistling. "Hey, lookit who Blackjack has!" "Yeah, look how he's duded up." "Hey, why didn't ya wear yer overalls, Blackjack?"

I blushed fourteen colors. Marie just kept walking and smiling.

The school orchestra struck up a Perry Como hit. Marie snaked a dainty arm around my neck and started dragging me across the floor. Her perfume smelled so strong I wanted to throw up. The guys were still bugging me. Not as loud as before, but calling as they came by: "Blackjack, yer 'sposed to hold her tighter than that." "Blackjack, don't stomp on yer sweetie's toes."

Marie now realized I couldn't dance. "Watch my feet," she whispered in my ear. "Follow me. One, two, three. That's it. You can do it, Blackjack. Hey, ouch, that's my foot. Careful, careful. One, two, three. Don't pull back. Ouch, that hurt!"

I could feel all the eyes on us. Two couples had completely stopped and were dying laughing. Splitting their sides.

"C'mon, Blackjack," Marie urged. "Let's move to the other side. Get away from these dummies who are making you so nervous.

"OK, one, two, three. Get in the rhythm. C'mon, you can do it. Ouch! Ouch! Oh, Blackjack, you're imposs—maybe we'd better sit down awhile."

We found a couple of empty chairs by the wall. When she turned to talk to another girl, I bolted for the door. The last I heard was this male voice: "Where ya goin', Blackjack? Come on back, the dance is jist gettin' started."

I didn't look back until I got safely inside the dorm. I don't recall that Marie ever spoke to me again.

What I really wanted was to play basketball. C.B. and Junior made the team. I tried out. Coach John Tucker, Tech's all-time great athletic hero, looked at me sadly. "You're OK at the free throw line, but in play you're just too little and skinny."

"Aw, Coach, gimme a chance?" I begged.

"Sorry, Son. My job is to win games. You'd be a drag on the team."

I sneaked onto the bus for the first road game. About twenty-five miles down the road, I wiggled out from under a rear seat. Somebody yelled, "Black-jack's with us. We're gonna be lucky tonight."

Coach Tucker called me to the front. He was not amused. "I've a good mind to put you off the bus and make you walk back."

"Aw, Coach. . . ."

"Let 'em stay with us, Coach," called a number of the players.

"Sit down, Hefley. I'll think about it."

His heart must have softened. When we stopped at a restaurant he handed me a meal ticket. I went on to the game and sat behind the bench. That was as close as I ever got to varsity sports.

I stayed at Tech for two quarters, and went home again in March 1945. I would not be fifteen until June and Mama and Daddy were glad to have me home. "You have lots of time," Mama said. "We can use your help in the store."

Every evening now the radio commentator Gabriel Heatter was saying, "There's good news tonight."

American B-29s bombed Tokyo.

American Marines took Iwo Jima and landed on Okinawa.

In Europe, the Allied Third Army crossed the Rhine while the Russian juggernaut rolled toward Berlin from the east.

The Rising Sun was sinking. Hitler was doomed.

But at terrible cost. The telegrams—"We regret to inform you . . ."—came by mail to Judy since there were no telephones. Cousin Lloyd had the solemn responsibility to hand them out. One reported that Wilson Strong, Clara Kent's nephew, had died on Iwo Jima. He and I had played together.

Still the war seemed unreal and so far away. Life in Judy crawled on the same. I slept late, fished, and helped a little in the store.

One morning I picked up the North mail at the post office. I thumbed through a catalog from a gambling supply house offering punchboards, slot machines, roulette wheels, gaming tables—the works. "We get our candy punchboards from them," Mama explained when she saw me looking at it.

I couldn't afford the big stuff, but how about "Jackpot Charley"? With a thousand punches at a quarter each, taking in $250 and paying out $200 in cash prices, it cost only $10. The wheels turned. Fifty dollars margin, less ten. Forty profit. How could I lose?

"Can I order one in the store's name?" I asked Mama.

She shrugged. "If you look after it. And pay the bill at the first of the month. We keep good credit with our suppliers."

"Sure, sure, and can I have the profit, then?"

Mama agreed. She didn't realize what I was getting into, or else she saw no difference between a money board and one that gave candy prizes.

I sent the order off and two weeks later the first money gambling device ever seen in Judy arrived. I propped the board on the candy counter Saturday morning and was open for business.

With the root and fur market and the stave bolt boom, there was money in Judy. A group gathered in minutes.

"Five dollar number!" Cousin Lonzo shouted. I had to borrow from the cash register to pay it off.

No need to worry. Lonzo punched ten dollars out trying to win one of the twenty-dollar prizes.

"Hey, let me try my luck." Another five dollar win and fifteen dollars' worth of business.

I hung over the counter, a stack of one-dollar bills in one hand and a box of quarters beside the other.

"Twenty dollars! Twenty smackeroos! Pay off, 'Fesser."

I counted out the money.

The punching became feverish. Two fellows tussled over the board. I grabbed it from their hands. "Take turnabout."

They punched ole Charley out in three hours, making me fifty dollars—less the ten I owed the company. Easy, sweet money.

I ordered three more Charleys, plus a nickel, dime, and even a dollar punchboard. Even after the novelty wore off, I still pulled in sixty to seventy dollars' profit every Saturday. By my fifteenth birthday, I was making more money some weeks than Mama and Daddy. I bought clothes, fishing reels and rods, lures, a portable typewriter, anything I wanted.

My gambling business was the most exciting thing going in Judy, until one Saturday afternoon a car bearing Illinois license tags drove into town. The store always emptied out when a strange vehicle arrived. I stayed by my punch boards, expecting the customers to return after satisfying their initial curiosity. When they didn't, I went to the door to see what was holding them.

A middleaged man and woman were coming into our store. The crowd was following two attractive teenage girls as they strolled through Judy—wearing white shorts!

Cousin Clyde came racing around the corner from Jones' Grocery. "Whar's them nekkid girls?"

Clyde and I ran to where Uncle Bill was questioning them in front of the cafe. The scantily clad females were giggling and obviously enjoying all the attention.

"Rosemary? Treela?" The woman was calling them from our store porch. The girls turned and sauntered back, their entourage of about fifty men and boys following.

The girls and the older couple walked across the road to the cobblestone house where the Johnsons had lived before moving to Springfield, Missouri.

"Who are they?" I asked Mama.

"Mr. and Mrs. Brandt from Illinois," she reported while eyeing the young women critically. "They're friends of Florence Billings and Marie Olsen, the missionaries from Hasty. They've rented the Johnsons' house. I guess the girls are their daughters."

Outsiders moving into Judy! Two teenage girls wearing shorts! That was all everybody talked about the rest of the day. Laughing about the girls, and speculating on why this Yankee family was moving to Judy. Someone suggested that since they knew the founders of the mission at Hasty, they might be missionaries too.

"Naw," came a reply. "I don't think missionaries would allow thar' young'uns to go half-nekkid in public."

They moved in the next week. It turned out that only the short girl was their daughter; the taller one was their niece and just visiting with them.

Rosemary, the petite one, was just thirteen, but pert and fiestier than a young filly. Her eyes bubbled with wonder and she giggled at everything I said. Her strange Yankee accent didn't put me off. She was a lot more to my liking than the pushy girls at Tech.

The Brandts weren't missionaries, but they were close enough. Pete, a thin, shy, gray-haired man in his early fifties, was a carpenter. His buxom wife, Hazel, talked to everyone within reach and struck up a special friendship with Mama. Next thing I knew she had invited us all to Bible study at her house, starting Sunday night.

Not many grown-ups were there. We boys filled the house, pushing and shoving to get closer to Rosemary and her cousin, Treela. Hazel finally had to call for order so Marie Olsen, who was leading the study, could be heard.

The crowd dwindled the next Sunday. Maybe the curiosity had just worn off. Maybe some of the parents didn't want their boys going to a "Baptist" Bible study. I didn't have any religious prejudice. In fact, I told Rosemary, "One of my best buddies at Tech is a Baptist." I didn't mention that Ole Red was a gambling buddy.

Uncle Bill's youngest son, Kenneth, was there. When I saw him shining up to Rosemary, I quickly got on the other side of her. She'd look at him and bat her eyes, then turn back to me and grin.

At this time a moving picture man was coming to Judy every Saturday night. He put up a tent and folding chairs beside the cafe and showed Hoot Gibson and Cisco Kid flicks. Uncle Bill and the old timers cheered their heroes on from the front row: "Go git 'em, Hoot!" "Look out, Cisco, he's got a gun."

"Would you like to go to the movie?" Kenneth and I said it so near the same time, Rosemary didn't know whom to answer.

Kenneth and I were second cousins and friends. We decided to be sensible and pitch a horseshoe game to see who would get the honor. Rosemary didn't believe us at first, but when she saw us the next day pitching in front of our house, she knew we were serious.

"Don't I have any say about who I go with?"

We both shook our heads.

"What if I don't go at all?"

"You'll go," I said confidently.

I took her the first Saturday night, Kenneth the next. This went back and forth, for we were both pretty good at horseshoes, with the winner walking her up the road to get a soda pop at the cafe, then walking her back home, and the loser hanging around close, just to be sure they behaved themselves.

Kenneth got a job in Little Rock and didn't come home for three weeks. Rosemary and I were already in the cafe when he showed up that Saturday night and called her outside. I followed and a crowd gathered.

"It's my turn to take her," he declared.

"Not my fault you haven't been here," I countered.

We went on arguing, the crowd getting bigger, some of the boys egging us on, hoping for a fight.

Rosemary put her hands on her hips and hollered, "Will everybody please shut up. I'm going to make the decision. Both Kenneth and James Carl are taking me to the movie. I like them both."

I could see that Kenneth didn't like that, but he went along, huffing and grumbling.

The Brandts moved back to Illinois. Many of my uncles and aunts were now leaving Big Creek Valley or preparing to do so. A good work hand could make forty dollars a week picking grapes in California, and even more working in a factory.

Junior Johnson, my classmate, had already married my Aunt Clara's sister and moved to Arvin, California. Aunt Clara and Uncle Loma, the constable, had located there also.

One morning I saw Daddy come in from feeding his dogs, looking glum.

"What's wrong, Fred?" Mama asked him.

"Haven't you heerd? Roy and Julia, Elmer and Viola, Lucy and Orvil, and their kids are all leaving for California tomorrow. They're going to look for Lomy and Clary."

"I heard them talking about it," Mama said. "Are they really going?"

"Reckon so."

Uncles Roy and Elmer were Daddy's brothers; Aunt Lucy, his sister. I would be losing at least seven first cousins—more if the older ones left with them.

Cousin Clyde, the balladeer and country blues singer of Judy, who sang us to sleep many nights with his rendition of Ernest Tubb's, "I'm Walkin' the Floor Over You," would be going. Also Cousins Athol, E.L., Marvin, Faman, Oral Lee, and Clayton.

They packed their belongings in boxes and flour sacks and loaded everything into Uncle Orvil's ton-and-a-half flatbed truck.

"Where will you sleep on the way?" Mama asked. Mama thought of things like that.

"We'll camp by the highway," Uncle Roy said. "We've got quilts and pillows and a tarpaulin to cover up with if'un it starts rainin'."

"What will you eat?"

"We're packing in enough baloney and crackers. We'll stop and buy sody pop at gay-us stations."

They piled in and Uncle Orvil started the motor. Cousin Clyde climbed atop the sideboard to wave good-bye. He held up his guitar. "I'll make some good music. They'll love us in Californy."

The truck roared out of sight, with my family and other kinfolks waving as long as we could see them.

We didn't hear a peep from them for five weeks. Then late one afternoon a truck stopped outside the store. "I'm walking the floor over you, I can't sleep a wink that is true. . . ."

Cousin Clyde! They were back.

Our whole family poured outside. There was a lot of confusion with everybody trying to talk at once. I caught Cousin Clyde's voice above all the rest: "Onct we stopped to get sumthin' to wet air whistles. Ole Marvin went in a cafe and axed fer one little ole glass of water. They charged him a dime! I wouldn't uf paid hit."

The questions were coming thick and fast.

"Did you find Lomy and Clary?"

"We drove up and down them fields around Arvin for three days and never did locate them," Uncle Roy reported. "We axed at all the fillin' stations, but nobody 'peared to know 'um. We picked ournges one day and got homesick and come on back."

"Didja have any tar' trouble?"

"W'ar thar lots of cars on the road?"

"How wuz the weather?"

"We had bald tires when we left and bald when we got back. Had only one flat."

"We seed lots and lots of cars, 'specially in Californy. We wuz so loaded that the only thang we passed wuz a terrapin."

"Hit wuz so hot in the back of the truck, we peeled off and blistered three times."

Judy settled down again. But even with the money coming from my punchboards, I got bored and decided another stretch at Tech couldn't be any worse.

With the war over, Tech was now on the semester system. The enrollment was heavy with veterans who loved to gamble and drink.

One night a big, chunky ex-Seabee named Harry and I outlasted all the rest. By around three in the morning I had every dollar in his billfold and was owed $180. He stood up and glowered at me. "I'll pay ya, Blackjack."

"When?" I wanted to know.

"When my ship comes in."

"When's that gonna be?"

"When I tell ya. Now, I'm goin' to bed."

His ship never did come in.

The gambling and drinking got real bad. I didn't drink. I just sat around while the other guys passed the bottle and waited until they were soused. Then I cleaned up. Gambling was in my blood. I was the first one out of the dorm for breakfast, challenging guys to pitch half dollars at cracks in the sidewalk. Afternoons, I hung out in the gym, wagering on basketball goals from the free throw line. Evenings, I was in the dorm lounge trying to get up a card game.

The administration sent down an edict to stop the gambling. We ignored it.

A few nights later, about two in the morning, I was dealing blackjack to about ten guys around a table in the lounge. Bills and coins were scattered across the table. I dealt a round and just happened to glance toward the door leading into the apartment where a faculty member lived. The creep was looking at us.

"Put up your cards and go to bed," he ordered. "I know who you are and I'm turning your names in to Coach Tucker."

Coach Tucker, who was also the dean of men, called a meeting of all Tech men in the dorm lounge. I purposely got there early and slouched down in a high-backed lounge chair turned so ole Tucker couldn't see me from the front.

He lectured us all about the drinking and gambling, then he named names. I was first on his list.

"Hefley, 'er, Blackjack, or whatever they call you, turn around and look at me."

I waved a hand.

A couple of guys laughed.

"Hefley, look at me!"

"Yeah. Here, Coach."

"Hefley, you are the worst influence on this campus. You're either going to shape up, or we'll ship you out. Understand?"

"Yeah."

"DID YOU HEAR ME? SAY, 'YES, SIR.'"

"YES, SIR."

Fortunately the semester was about done. I didn't need Tech. I went home and ordered a new supply of punchboards. I got a slot machine, the first ever seen in Newton County. It was my sixteenth birthday present to myself.

I was there behind the candy counter, tending to my gambling business, when I spied a letter to Mama from Hazel Brandt. I don't usually open other people's mail, but this one I did. Hazel said they were moving back to Judy and that she was "praying James Carl will get saved."

"Stupid!" I muttered aloud. "I don't need any religion."

But I was glad Rosemary would be back.

She was a year older and prettier than ever. But she was so sassy! In Judy a female didn't talk back to a male. This one did—to me.

"You've turned into a smart aleck, James Carl," she said. "I don't like that."

"Takes one to know one," I muttered and jumped up, slamming the door as I ran out.

She apologized. I said I was sorry, too.

The next time was worse. Her mama heard us yelling at one another and ran from the kitchen to see what was the matter.

Rosemary stomped her foot. "I can't stand him."

"I'm sick of you," I shouted.

"Sit down, both of you," Hazel ordered. "I've been hearing you two argue day after day. It's time something was done about it. Now you can be friends, but you're both too young to be dating. Wait until you grow up."

I avoided the Brandt house for the next three or four days. I caught sight of Rosemary walking to Judy School a time or two, but I didn't speak.

Then I met her outside her house one evening. "Your mama was right," I said. "We are too young."

She agreed.

"But I really do like you, no matter what." I reached for her hand.

"And I like you, James Carl. I'm sorry that we're moving again."

"What? Where? When?"

"Daddy has a job in Houston. He's already down there and is coming back for us tomorrow."

I didn't quite know how to respond. Finally I whispered, "Let's go sit on your swing."

"Sure. Let's."

A pale moon hung low over Judy. A cow lumbered along in front of the stores, raising barks from Daddy's hounds. A Model-A clattered by. Then all was still except for the soft, rhythmic squeak of the swing. I curled an arm around her shoulder. We swung there, kicking our legs in unison, content.

"Will you write me?"

"Yes, and I want to hear from you."

"Rosemary? R-o-s-e-m-a-r-y? ROSEMARY?"

"Out here, Mother."

"It's too cold out there. Come on in."

I walked her the few steps to the door. We pressed hands and said goodnight.

Her family migrated from Houston back to Illinois and stayed. She married a hometown boy named Loyal who became an accountant. They moved to Los Angeles and had two daughters.

I kept up with her family through her mother's letters to my mother. On a business trip to Los Angeles, I decided to call. After all, we had both been happily married to our own spouses for twenty years.

She and Loyal invited me over. I wondered what she would look like. Honestly, I wouldn't have recognized her. She was still good looking, but in a different, more sophisticated way.

Loyal and I became instant friends. I felt comfortable with him. We looked at pictures of my family. He laughed with us as Rosemary and I shared old times.

"I'm still mad about you and Kenneth pitching horseshoes to see who would take me to the picture show," she said, with a flash of the old fire in her eyes. "The audacity of you two! And I haven't forgotten the fusses we had." She laughed.

"We didn't get along very well," I recalled.

"Oh, James Carl, that's bygones. We were just kids. By the way, how is Kenneth? I heard he married a girl named Maxine, and they live in Little Rock and have some boys."

"You haven't heard?"

"Heard what?"

"A few days after Kenneth was promoted to supervisor of his company, he was burned to death in a gas explosion in his basement. None of his family was hurt."

Rosemary put her hand to her mouth in shock. "Oh, how terrible! Poor Maxine and the boys. Oh, I'm so sorry."

"I was shocked when I heard it. I lost a cousin and a good friend."

Rosemary and Loyal's two daughters arrived. Loyal took us all out to dinner. As we were eating pies, Rosemary brought up Kenneth again.

"We were just kids," she repeated, "but I'll never forget him. And you. And our growing up years in Judy."

"Neither will I," I echoed.

FIFTEEN
I Know Who I Am

Early on Wednesday morning I was sitting on the store porch, kidding around with O. J. George and Billy Wayne Humes. O. J., a very distant cousin, was Judy's unofficial clown and stunt man. He'd come riding into Judy on his old bay horse, whooping and hollering, making you think he was going to run you over. Then, just in the nick of time, he'd pull back on the reins, the horse would rear up, and he'd slide off the back end and into the dirt. Billy Wayne was more of a muscle man, big and beefy, the guy you wanted on your side in a fight. With O. J. the clown prince, me the straight man, and Billy Wayne, the enforcer, we made quite a trio.

"Hey, looky thar." O. J. pointed to an old car that rattled to a stop in front of the store.

We watched two well-dressed young women in their twenties step out, one blonde and freckled, the other dark-haired. We sat there grinning as they walked over to us.

"Good morning, fellows," the blonde said in a crisp foreign accent.

O. J. covered his sputtering mouth. Billy Wayne punched me on the shoulder. "Speak to the Yankees, 'Fesser. Be a gentleman."

I coughed a weak greeting.

"I'm Florence Handyside and my partner here is Helen Lievie. We're new missionaries with Marie Olsen and Florence Billings' group. Fellows, we want to hold young people's meetings in the school on Monday evenings. We need permission from the chairman of your school board, a Mr. William Hefley. Could you direct us to him?"

I stood up and pointed to the old man snoozing in a hickory-bottomed chair on the post office porch. "That's Uncle Bill. But you'll have to wake him up."

Our three pairs of eyes followed the Yankee women up the road. We saw the one named Florence nudge Uncle Bill gently. We couldn't hear what they were saying but we guessed Uncle Bill was giving them his usual line of questioning. After a long time they came back all smiles.

"Fellows," Florence said, "Uncle Bill has given permission for us to use the school. You and all the young people in town are invited. Will you get the word around? We'll play games and sing and have Bible stories. You'll enjoy it."

I glanced over at O. J. and Billy Wayne and winked. "We'll be there," I pledged. I punched Billy Wayne in the ribs and jumped back to escape his blow. "And Bill here will see that the others come."

The three of us had a ball every Monday night: Teasing, punching, scuffling, pulling chairs from under boys, dropping beetles down girls' backs. When they started the music, we sang off key. When they asked for selections, Billy Wayne called out, "The Old Rugged Cross" every single week.

I kept expecting these Yankee gals to grab a broom and whack us over the head. Instead, they just said: "Fellows, please sit down." "O. J., could you do that stunt some other time?" "James Carl, we know you can sing better than that." "Billy Wayne, could you save your strength to help us straighten the room afterwards?"

After the singing, if you could call it that, Florence gave a Bible lesson. The three of us yammered while she was talking. I had heard the Bible argued in Judy all my life. I had even taken a credit Old Testament course at Tech, taught by a Russellville pastor, and made an A. The only A on my record. I didn't need to be taught religion by two Yankee women.

Judy was pretty dull then. Cousin Clyde's family had gone back to California and this time found Uncle Loma and Aunt Clara. The only event of the week, besides the Church of Christ Sunday school—which I never attended—was Florence and Helen's young people's meeting. Bill, O. J., and I had our fun every Monday night until finally our tomfoolery got boring. I mean, how many times can you pull a chair out from under Cousin Billy Buck and have it be funny?

What puzzled and even exasperated me was the patience of Florence and Helen. They never once exploded at us.

Heavy rains brought high water. The north mail didn't get through for a week. Monday night without Florence and Helen seemed empty. I wouldn't admit it to anyone, but I liked those gals.

We speculated as to whether they would come the next week, for the creeks were up again, though not as much as before. About dark their old car came clattering and coughing into the school yard.

Florence opened the door and stepped out barefooted and smiling. "Only the Lord could have brought us through the creeks. The water ran through the floorboards, and we drowned out once. Somebody must have been praying."

I picked up their flannel board and bag of song books. Billy Wayne packed in the accordion which Florence played as accompaniment. O. J. ran up and offered to help. We were in a different mood that night.

I felt pity for Florence and Helen. Leaving their comfortable homes and coming to Newton County where few showed them any appreciation. Putting up with our foolishness week after week. Taking a chance on having their car ruined in the creeks. And for what? It certainly wasn't money. I had once overheard Hazel Brandt telling Mama that the Hasty missionaries were not on salary, but "just looked to God and friends back home to provide." Hazel had taken a meal at the mission house and seen what little they had to eat.

That was a very melancholy evening. Few came, thinking Florence and Helen wouldn't brave the creeks. Because the group was so small, we sat around talking about ourselves. Finally I asked Florence and Helen to tell us a little about themselves.

Florence said she was from New York, Helen from Pennsylvania. They became friends at Moody Bible

Institute where both had taken the foreign mission course.

"This is foreign missions?" I asked.

"Well, kind of." Florence laughed. "Our mission boards require some practical experience before we're ready to go overseas."

"We're your experience?"

"Yes. Pretty good experience, I'd say," Helen replied, and they both laughed.

The next Monday night they started a study of the life of Christ. Florence positively glowed as she talked. "Can you imagine, God becoming a man, like one of us? A servant? A sacrifice for our sins? This God who created the universe and millions of stars and planets and solar systems. This God who will one day ring down the curtain of history. Can you imagine?"

I listened respectfully. I was feeling a little guilty for causing Florence and Helen so much trouble. But my mind kept saying, *Same old stuff. You've heard it all your life. You're too smart to believe it.*

Yes, but it sounded different this time.

"You think you're too good or too smart to believe?" How had Florence known what I was thinking?

"The real problem for some of you may be that you're just too chicken to look and see if it could be true." Florence was looking straight at me.

Yeah, but suppose I do want to know? What church do I join? Whose doctrines do I accept?

"Are you asking, 'Where do I begin?' Well, you don't start by arguing over doctrines. You start with Jesus. You ask God, 'Show me if Jesus is all he claimed to be.' Then you listen to what the Bible says about Jesus. You listen with an open mind.

"Jesus said in John 7:17, 'If any man will do his will, he shall know.' That's a promise. But you must be willing."

I don't need your Jesus Christ. I'm as good as any of the church people; better than some. I don't drink or cuss or take girls into the woods as some guys do. Maybe I gamble, but I play by the rules.

"Forget about other people. Don't fall into the trap of comparing your own life with someone else's. If you hide behind a hypocrite, you're smaller than he is."

Uncanny.

"OK, we're beginning our study of Jesus. I suggest you draw a circle about yourself. Ask yourself, what does Jesus say to me?"

A speck of light began to dawn. I had made certain assumptions about God, the Bible, Jesus, and religion. I had been judgmental and self-righteous. I had never bothered—dared to open up and consider Jesus and myself.

I'll listen. And when you're done, I'll be the same as before.

Week by week, Florence and Helen took us through the life of Christ, from the Old Testament prophecies of his coming to his New Testament birth, miracles, teachings, death, resurrection, and promised return. I took it all in. Slowly I opened to the possibility that Jesus might be the Son of God. If he wasn't, then he was either crazy or a liar with a lot of imagination. Neither characterization seemed to fit. How could a crazy person, or a pathological liar speak such majestic words as the Sermon on the Mount?

They reached the end of the study. Florence announced they would be moving on to Lurton. The next Monday night would be their last time in Judy.

Who could blame them? Every Monday evening, at the close of the talk, they had us sing a song, during which they invited those who would accept Jesus as Savior and Lord to come and stand at the front of the room with them. No one ever moved an inch.

Their last meeting came. Florence looked at us and smiled. "God loves you. He came as Jesus and died on the cross for your sins. He calls you to accept him, to take your stand for him, to declare that you love him and want to follow him."

Helen started the song,

Softly and tenderly Jesus is calling,
Calling for you and for me. . . .

Florence held out her arms. "Come and trust in Jesus. Tonight. Come. Come."

I glanced across at Billy Wayne, nervously drumming a finger on the desk. I looked over at O. J. I caught the eye of Cousin Billy Buck. Nobody moved.

See on the portals he's waiting and watching,
Watching for you and for me.
Come home, come home. . . .

"Come home to Jesus tonight," Florence pleaded.

I looked down at my feet. *You're getting to me. I'm not going to fall for this. I'll not have guys making fun. I'm too smart. One religion is as good as another. Some of the best people I know are not religious. Riley. Grandpa Pulliam.*

"Bow your heads as we close in prayer."

I exhaled a sigh of relief.

I never saw Florence and Helen again. I heard that they moved to Lurton and lived in a one-room shack with cracks so big that snow blew onto their beds in winter. Then they left Newton County and, we presumed, became foreign missionaries.

I continued to tend my punchboards and slot machine. Late one Saturday afternoon, Troy Tennison, a very distant cousin and an ex-Marine, lost $40. His mama learned about it and was outraged. She went to see Sheriff Burdine.

"Ain't commercial gambling illegal in this county?"

He allowed that it was.

"Why do you let Fred Hefley's boy stay in business?"

"Aw, he jist makes a few nickels and dimes. If I tried to stop everybody betting on something, I'd be doing nothing else."

"You've been too busy with them moonshiners to know whut's goin' on, Russell. James Carl Hefley took forty dollars from my boy. He also has a slot machine. Did ye know that?"

Russell's brows furrowed. "No, I didn't. But I'll take care of your problem."

Russell sent my folks a warning that he was "coming over tomorrow to check on a complaint that your boy is running a gambling business."

Mama came to me all flustered. She was afraid we might be fined—or worse, I might be put in jail.

I know it seems contradictory that Mama had allowed this, with her strict moral code and stern opposition to drinking. But she honestly didn't see that gambling was hurting anybody. Perhaps because she just couldn't visualize one of *her* kids doing wrong.

"Not to worry," I told Mama. "I'll hide the stuff so he can't find it."

I did and went fishing the next day. Russell came and looked around the store. He bought a nickel soda pop, chatted a few minutes with Mama about kinfolks and the weather, then asked about me.

"He's gone fishing, Russell," she said. "You know how he likes to fish."

"Well, I've had a complaint about his little gambling enterprise. If I git another one, I mou't have ta take somebody to Jasper."

"I'll talk to him, Russell. He's a good boy."

"Sure, sure, I know he is. Just don't let me hear that he's running them punchboards and that slot machine."

The whole thing really ticked me off. Who was this woman to interfere with my business? Who was Russell Burdine to tell me what I could and couldn't do? I'd show them!

After laying out for a year, I picked up my studies at Tech, taking accounting, economics, and business management. I figured on finishing up in another year and moving on to Las Vegas or Reno where gambling was legal. One day I would have my own casino where the busybodies couldn't get at me. I'd come back to Judy driving a Cadillac and wearing three-hundred-dollar suits. I'd buy the whole dad-blamed town and the county sheriff to boot!

This time I buckled down to my studies and cut out the six-hour blackjack and poker sessions. I was even invited to church by my old gambling buddy, who was active in the Baptist Student Union.

"Man, you've gotta be kiddin'," I responded. "The roof would fall in."

I had a couple of problems. My second cousin "Gander," Lloyd's James Carl, was now enrolled at Tech. Since both had the same name, our records were getting mixed up. "I'm the younger," I told him. "I'll just add 'Jr.' to my name."

The other problem could not be solved so easily. It was like low-grade infection in my mind, an irritation forcing me to ponder some heavy thoughts.

What if I make a pile of money in gambling, I have a family, I die. Then what? Am I just dropped into a grave to rot and return to the earth? Is that all there is?

Suppose there is a heaven and hell. Suppose the Bible isn't a pack of myths. Suppose Jesus Christ is God.

A verse quoted by Florence jabbed me in the teeth: *"I am the way, the truth, and the life; no man comes to the Father but by me."*

Ridiculous! What about Muhammad, Buddha, and all the rest?

Then Jesus must be a liar, deluded, or crazy. Or the Bible writer put words in his mouth.

What if he really is God?

Do I really want to know?

In this frame of debate, I went home for spring break. Between the sucker and bass seasons, the fishing was blah. I was afraid to put out the punch-boards and slot machine. I sat around the store, pitched horseshoes, read, argued in my mind with Florence and Helen, remembering their incredible patience and love.

Saturday evening, I was pitching horseshoes. Mama came out about dark and said, "Son, a Preacher Denny is holding services in our living room tonight. Won't you please come in and hear him?"

We owned the old "hotel" then, which was no more than an oversized residence. Mama had beds there and also behind the partition in the store. She cooked at the store and the family slept there most of the time. When I came home I usually stayed in the hotel alone.

"Aw, Mama, look how dirty I am."

"You've got time to wash your hands and face. Nobody cares if you come in your overalls. Come on, Son, please."

Mama was a pleader and a wheedler. "OK, Mama, I'll be in after this game."

I slipped quietly through the front door and eased up the stairs that led to my sleeping room. Halfway up I remembered my promise to Mama and sat down. About twenty people were sitting around the room. I knew them all, except the bespectacled little man in a black suit. Mama and Daddy were there. That was something. I hadn't seen them in a church service since the White House School.

They sang a few songs and the preacher stood up with his big black Bible.

Let him preach. If he gets to buggin' me, I'll go on up the stairs and to bed.

Preacher Denny began warm and friendly, cracking jokes, making remarks about different people in Judy he had met. A likable guy. I relaxed. Then he got into sin and judgment, hellfire and brimstone. I sat transfixed, unable to move.

The Bible says, 'All have sinned.' All. A double l. Everybody. You. Me. The Bible says, 'The heart is deceitful and desperately wicked.' Your heart. My heart. 'Deceitful.' Crooked. The Bible says, 'It is appointed unto man once to die and after that the judgment.' Everybody will die. You will. You won't escape God's judgment. He'll call you to the bar.

"Thank God, there's a way of escape. He came and died on a cross for your sins. Now you don't have to understand that. You just know that you're a sinner and trust in him. You claim his forgiveness. You say, 'Yes, Lord, I believe. I accept.'

"Oh, ho. Is there somebody here who thinks he doesn't need this forgiveness? Somebody who thinks he's better than everybody else?"

Yeah, I'm that one. I don't drink, cuss, smoke, or chase girls for the wrong reasons. But I'm greedy, selfish. I don't like to share. I like to take money from people. I want to get rich off people.

"Man, will you be fooled. The Lord will line you up and start counting out your sins. You'll call on the rocks and mountains to fall on you and save you from the wrath to come."

All that Florence and Helen had said came rolling in on me like a flood. Dadnab it, I had to admit the truth.

I am a sinner. I do need to be saved.

Preacher Denny introduced a song familiar from Florence and Helen's meetings. Everyone stood and began singing:

> *Just as I am without one plea,*
>   *But that Thy blood was shed for me,*
> *And that Thou bidst me come to Thee,*
>   *O Lamb of God, I come, I come. . . .*

The preacher was holding out his arms. "Come and take my hand and say you'll trust Jesus as your Savior. Come tonight, now."

I stood up and looked at my dirty hands. I hadn't bothered to wash. My clothes were dirty. My *heart* was dirty.

My heart was also pounding, my palms sweating.

I gotta be cool and rational, I argued to myself.

Yeah, and reject the Lord again.

I can make this decision some other time.

You don't know there will be another time.

I need to understand more.

You know that you're a sinner and that God loves you. That's enough.

Something within me gave way. I stumbled down those stairs, a tall, ungainly sixteen-year-old boy, and reached for the preacher's hand. He came rushing to meet me.

"I believe . . . I believe that Jesus died for me," I croaked, my eyes rimming with tears.

"You're trusting Jesus as your Savior? You're taking your stand for him?"

"Yes. I am."

"What's your name, son?"

"James Carl Hefley." I pointed to Daddy. "I'm his son."

The preacher turned me around to face the people. "Praise God, Fred's boy is trusting in Jesus!"

Mama was crying. Daddy, too. The first time I had ever seen him shed a tear.

Preacher Denny had a prayer with me. Then he shook everybody's hand and came back to say he would see me in a few days. "Meantime, read the New Testament, Son. Learn all you can about Jesus."

I went upstairs and slept like a log. The next morning the birds sang sweeter, the trees looked greener, the honeysuckles smelled more fragrant than ever before. I stepped livelier, felt better, and saw people through happier eyes.

I read the New Testament and loved it. It was astonishing how much I hadn't known about Jesus and the apostles.

Preacher Denny returned early one Saturday morning when I was home again from Tech. I was still in bed, but awake and reflecting on the decision I had made two weeks before. We talked a few minutes, then he said "Boy, you've got a good case of salvation. Praise the Lord! Boy, I think the Lord may be calling you to be a preacher."

"I think so, too." The words just popped out of my mouth.

"We're beginning a Baptist Sunday school a week from Sunday in the Brandts' old house. How about giving the devotion?"

"What's a devotion?"

"Oh, you just pick a Scripture and talk on it for about five minutes. You can do it."

The devotion was no sweat. I always could talk in front of people.

For some reason Cousin Goober thought I was going to preach. He peeked in the window to see. After Sunday school, he caught me and said, "You didn't preach. You just talked a little."

Preacher Denny went on to another appointment. That afternoon I got bored and went fishing. Coming back with a nice string of bass, I met Goober.

"You a preacher and fishing on Sunday?"

I grunted guiltily and walked on home. Preacher Denny already had appointments set up for me to preach at Deer, Ben Hur, and Jasper in Newton County. I typed out a bunch of Scripture verses on my little portable Underwood. I read them from the pulpit and made comments in between. The folks at Deer and Ben Hur bragged that I was the best young preacher they had ever heard. Of course, they hadn't heard many my age. Maybe none at all.

My left shoe sole came loose the day I went to Jasper. Mama didn't believe in but one pair of shoes a year, and since folding my gambling business I hadn't been able to afford a new pair.

Mama and Daddy went with me to the county seat for the Sunday evening service. The Baptists were meeting in the stone Methodist Church while their church was under construction. The floor was slick and shiny, the pews straight and hard, the pulpit big and fancy. I made the mistake of sitting with my parents on the last pew.

When the man introduced me I got up and made my first step toward the front. *Flip*, smacked the sole of my shoe. I took another step. *Flop*. The church was half empty, lending an echo effect. *Flip, flop. Flip, flop.* When I reached the pulpit I wanted to crawl in the back and hide.

Mama said afterwards, "Son, I think you need a new pair of shoes."

I had forgotten all about my gambling equipment. Returning home, I remembered. The next morning I took the punchboards and the slot machine from their hiding place. I carried them out behind the hotel and smashed them with the ax. When I finished, you couldn't tell a bar from a bell.

Preacher Denny paid my way to the Arkansas Baptist Youth Assembly near Siloam Springs in the far northwest corner of the state. The bus dropped me beside the highway at the entrance to the assembly grounds. I looked down into a little valley dotted with rustic dorms, a swimming pool, a dining hall, and a big open-air tabernacle. Kids about my age swarmed everywhere. I suddenly realized I didn't know a soul.

That didn't last long. Three guys grabbed me at the entrance: Glendon Grober, T. W. Hunt, and John McClanahan. One of them plopped a sailor's hat on my head and announced that I was on their team—the Goslings—for the afternoon sports contest. Before the week's fun and inspiration were done, I was pledged to join them that fall at Ouachita Baptist College in Arkadelphia, seventy-miles south of Little Rock.

At Siloam Springs I had been challenged to share my faith personally. When I got back to Judy I borrowed Daddy's pickup truck and drove up the mountain to see Grandpa Pulliam.

"GRANDPA, DO YOU LOVE JESUS?"

"Whut, James Carl? Speak a little louder."

"GRANDPA, DO YOU TRUST JESUS AS YOUR SAVIOR?"

"Reckon I do."

That was as far as I got with Grandpa.

I talked with my brother, Howard Jean. He squirmed around and wouldn't look at me directly. Finally he said, "Aw, shore, 'Fesser, I b'lieve in God and all that. Let's go fishin'."

When the word got around that I had joined up with Preacher Denny's crowd, I began having visitors.

Uncle Bill: "See, ole son, Paul wrote to the Romans, chapter sixteen and verse sixteen, 'The churches of Christ salute ye.' He didn't say 'Baptist churches,' did he, old son? Now ye take baptism. The baptists say it ain't necessary for salvation. Now we read in Acts, chapter two and verse thirty-eight. . . ."

Several texts later: "See, ole son, if you won't listen to Scripture, you oughter 'member that ye're a Hefley. Most of us Hefleys worship with the true church, the one that wuz thar 'fore all them Baptists and Holiness folks got started. I hope ye'll consider all this 'fore ye let that Preacher Denny baptize ye."

Uncle Dan: "W'al, now, James Carl, we'uns in the Holiness would lak ye to come with us. Course, I ain't got nuthin' 'ginst them Baptists. Tha'r good people, mighty fine. Us'ta be one, myself. But they don't tell ye how to git the Holy Ghost."

Nevertheless, I lined up to be baptized by Preacher Denny in the lower end of the Henry Hensley Hole, where I had cast so many times for bass. Then Mama and Daddy drove me to the bus station in Harrison.

"You be careful changing buses in Little Rock," Mama warned. "Watch out for thieves and robbers in the bus station. Keep your billfold pocket buttoned. And don't go wanderin' off and miss your bus."

She cried. Daddy shook my hand and said, "God bless ye, we'll be thinkin' of ye." I swung aboard the bus and was gone.

T. W. Hunt saw me in the registration line at Ouachita. "Welcome, fellow Gosling." He smiled. Johnny McClanahan and Glendon Grober came up and said how glad they were to see me. Other boys and also some girls I had met at Siloam Springs gave me the glad hand. I felt wanted.

Mama and Daddy had given me enough money for room and board. I took a janitor's job to pay for tuition. This meant climbing out of bed at five-thirty to get a building ready for classes. T. W. saw me coming down a hall with a broom and asked, "How do ya like Ouachita?"

"Great," I said laughing, "except I've learned it doesn't pay well to serve Jesus. I did much better in the gambling business."

I decided to join the National Guard to make a few extra bucks drilling one night a week. For that I had to write for a birth certificate.

Little Rock said they had no record of me being born. I wrote Mama for information and she replied that I should write to Ohio. "You'll understand when you get your record," was her only explanation.

The birth certificate from Ohio said I was Frederick Joseph Hefley. My Daddy's occupation was listed as "Federal Prisoner, U.S.I. Reformatory."

You could have knocked me over with a sunflower seed. I thought I knew everything about my family, and now this! What was he in for? What had Mama been doing up there? I didn't want to write and there was still no telephone in Judy. I'd wait until I went home for a visit.

The National Guard admitted me, but the clerk advised, "You ought to get your name straightened out sometime." I couldn't afford a lawyer and I had come this far as James Carl, so why not keep it that way? At least I was a Hefley.

I waited until I got Mama and Daddy together with nobody listening in. Mama did most of the talking and told me their long-kept secret. The year after they were married, when Daddy was still eighteen, an older man told them about an easy way to order merchandise from a mail-order house. "List what you want on the order, then fill out and sign a name. to a bank check for that amount and mail it in. The company will send you the goods before the check goes through the bank."

Seven Newton County folks, four men and three women, were involved in this little scheme. Daddy was the youngest. They were all caught, except the ringleader. He promised to take care of their families if they would plead guilty and keep quiet about his part.

Because they had used the mails to defraud, they appeared before the Federal judge in Harrison. He sentenced the older men to Leavenworth. Daddy and another man were given short terms in the U.S. Industrial Reformatory in Chillicothe, Ohio. The women got off with probation.

"I was in the family way for you," Mama said, "when your Daddy was taken off to jail. Things were mighty hard on Honey Creek then. When your Daddy wrote, begging me to come up there, I decided to go.

"My kinfolks bought me a ticket and put me on the train at Bergman. I got off the train in St. Louis to transfer and fainted beside the tracks. Some kind people found me there, looked at my ticket, and carried me to the right train, where I revived.

"The head guard felt sorry for us, your daddy being so young and me going to have a baby. He said I could stay and help his sick wife while he was at work. Your daddy and I could see each other once a week.

"James Carl, you were born in a second-story bedroom in the guard's house. You had a big knot on your head and didn't appear to be breathing. We all thought you were dead until the doctor picked you up and spanked your behind. You let out the awfulest and most blessed squall I ever heard.

"You don't hold all this against us, do you, Son? I reckon everybody makes mistakes. We never did it again."

I took my dear parents by the hands. "Mama, Daddy, it makes me feel proud to think that you didn't let that keep you from building a good name and raising eight children with so much love."

"I just don't want you holding it against us."

"Well, I don't, and I don't think anybody else will, either."

I asked them about my different names. "Oh, I reckon the doctor put Frederick Joseph on the birth certificate," Mama said. "We named you James Carl."

I felt relieved. "James Carl is who I want to be," I said. "What's in a name? Besides, it's being a Hefley that's important. Knowing I'm part of the family. Feeling I belong. Knowing all my kinfolks. That's the important thing."

With the name snafu cleared, I went on to graduate from Ouachita in 1950. My Bachelor of Arts diploma, with a major in Bible and a minor in Literature, was made out to James Carl Hefley.

The years passed swiftly. Seminary in New Orleans. Marriage to Marti. I signed the wedding certificate Frederick Joseph James Carl Hefley, Jr., just to be sure. The preacher saw it and cracked, "Hmmmmn, that looks like bigamy."

Eight years were spent as an urban preacher in New Orleans. Two-and-one-half years as an editor of a church magazine in Illinois. Eighteen years as a writer. Three children and two grandchildren.

Then came a surprising call from Dr. Daniel Grant, President of Ouachita, stating the trustees had voted to award me the honorary Doctor of Letters at the spring commencement, 1981.

Mama and Daddy and my brothers and sisters got special invitations. Dear Mama, soon to be diagnosed as having the dread Alzheimer's disease, scarcely knew what was happening. The night before the ceremony she kept waking up in the motel room, saying, "Fred. Fred. Where are we?"

Ottis and Onata Denny came all the way from Ohio, where Ottis was retired from his ministry as a Baptist church planter. Many of my old classmates were there. I shared the spotlight with Glendon Grober, who had been brought back from Brazil to be given an honorary Doctor of Divinity for his dynamic missionary leadership. Neither Glendon nor I knew the other was to be honored until we saw our pictures on the front page of the local paper the night before.

President Grant asked me to speak briefly before the degree was conferred. It was impossible to name them all, but I tried to pay tribute to the people who had influenced my life. Mama and Daddy. Grandparents, especially Grandpa Pulliam. Teachers, particularly Clara Kent. Roommates and classmates, including Glendon, John, and T. W.

In a distinctive category: Ottis Denney, Florence Billings, Hazel Brandt, Marie Olsen, who had recently died from cancer, and Helen Lievie, now a missionary in India. And Florence Handyside. . . . I had recently found out some things about her.

I took a deep breath to keep control. "Florence came to Newton County to prepare to be a missionary. She and her co-worker held youth meetings at the Mount Judea School every Monday night for almost a year. Not one of us kids ever responded.

They moved to Lurton and lived in a drafty shack and had little response there. Florence went to Korea and was stricken by polio just as she was beginning her foreign missionary service.

"Florence never knew that I, one of her chief troublemakers, became a Christian, or that other members of my family accepted the Lord. She never knew on earth, but surely she must now know in heaven.

"I am here today because of these people and many more."

President Grant read the citation, ending, "It is a special pleasure to confer this degree upon Ouachita's distinguished son, James C. Hefley."

The crowd of four thousand stood and applauded. Mama turned to my sisters and asked, "Why are they clapping?"

"For your oldest son, Mama. It's for James Carl."

Mama now lies in a nursing home, thin and white-faced, her hair a shiny silver, her deep-set eyes staring into space. Her hands shake, her chin quivers, for she also has Parkinson's.

I stand by her side and softly call, "Mama, Mama."

Her eyes turn slowly.

"Mama?"

She's trying to place me in her world.

"You're one of my boys. Howard Jean?"

"No, Mama, James Carl."

"Ah, James Carl. Come and let me kiss you."

Daddy is having a tough time adjusting to her dread illnesses. He stays with first one child, then another. With Mama as she is, he does not care to hunt anymore.

One more time I return to Big Creek and drive up the new road built along the hillside to avoid the fords. I stop and visit with Cousin Wilsie, daughter of Uncle Elmer, and her husband Beecher Cook. They and their children now own all of the upper valley, which they use for a hog and cattle ranch.

Wilsie gazes across the panorama of stream and fields below us. "This valley was once full of people. Now we're the only ones left."

I drive on to Grandpa Hefley's place. I stand on the porch of the 125-year-old house that the Cooks now use for a hay barn. I think of the good times here, the funerals, the generations gone before.

I climb the hill to the place where I lived until I was nine. A heap of fireplace stones and the rock wall that stood behind the kitchen are all that remain. The barn is gone, except for some foundation stones. The spring is mossed over.

But the graveyard is still there and the tombstone to further remind me of who I am, the namesake of "Natty" Jim Hefley.

There's a little postscript about Grandpa Jim. While I was researching my ancestry for this book, the old fellow gave me another shock.

Aunt Ellen Hefley, then the oldest surviving member of my clan, told me in a nursing home just before she died: "Jim was jist a little ole boy who Grampa Harv and Grandma Adaline took in. I never knew who his mama and daddy w'ar. I don't think they wuz Hefleys."

I called Marti at home to give her this astounding news and said, "If true, this blows my research in

Hefley genealogy. But I'm going to do some more digging."

"Well, let me know when you find out who you are."

I asked Cousin Custer, whose mother was Daddy's oldest sister. "Mama told us before she died that Grandpa Jim was an O'Neal," he said.

I delivered that information to Marti.

The next evening I called her back with a different story. "Others in the family think the name was Hale. There's one theory that Grandpa Jim's mother was a young woman named Minerva Jane Hefley who went back to Kentucky after his birth.

"It's really confusing. First I discovered that my name is Frederick Joseph on my birth certificate. Now it seems I'm not even from the Hefley line."

"Oh, don't worry, Honey," my wife comforted me with a lilt in her voice. "I love you, whoever you are!"

"Thank you," I replied. "But I do know who I am. I'll always be the oldest son of Fred and Hester Hefley. The grandson of Tom and Eller Hefley and Pulliam and Barbara Foster. The great-grandson of Jim and. . . ."

"Enough! You've convinced me." She laughed.

"And I'm also a child of God by the second birth."

"Amen," she declared.

AMEN and AMEN.

AFTERWORD/ APPRECIATIONS

My wife, Marti, was researching a book in a tribal area of the Philippines while I was laying the groundwork for this book. "Why do you want to talk to me?" a self-effacing little dark-skinned man asked her in Mindanao. "I'm just from a little hill tribe in the mountains."

"Oh, don't worry about that," she replied. "My husband is from one of the hill tribes in the United States."

Truly we are all tribals. I am proud to be from a hill tribe in Newton County, Arkansas. I am proud of the ancestry and heritage in which my identity was formed.

This is the story of me and my tribe. It is neither genealogy nor biography. It is simply a looking back to the good times and bad times and the dear people who shaped my life.

The sources are my own memory and the remembrances of kin and friends who shared the experience of growing up on Big Creek. Taped interviews and notes comprise over 400 single-spaced pages of transcripts. These materials are buttressed by historical documentation from old census rolls, deeds, marriage licenses, and war records.

I have sought to be both honest and understanding, straightforward and sympathetic. The triumphs are narrated along with the defeats. I may be faulted by some for presenting too dark a picture and rattling family skeletons; others may think I have been too charitable. To the first I plead that I cannot be phony before kith and kin. To the second I answer that we hillbillies have been unfairly stereotyped and stigmatized in big media.

Only my wife and our daughter Cheri, the much appreciated typist, have read this manuscript. I felt that if I shared it with one relative or old friend, I must share it with them all. None can thus be blamed for what is herein.

The events happened, although I have exercised some degree of literary license in reproducing conversations of the past. Beware of any writer who tells you he can remember verbatim such dialogue. However, in many instances I have presented quotations just as they were spoken. For example, the dialogue from "Lum and Abner" is taken from actual broadcasts, preserved for posterity.

The people are real. I have used a few pseudonyms, mainly in the chapter "That 'Good' Ole Mountain Dew," the reason being not to cause anyone embarrassment.

I thank all who shared remembrances: Mama (before her mind was crippled by Alzheimer's), Daddy, brothers and sisters, cousins, aunts and uncles, old friends and new friends.

I thank the helpful folks at the Arkansas State Historical Commission, as well as kind librarians in Jackson, Lawrenceburg, and Alamo, Tennessee; in Harrison, Arkansas; at Arkansas Tech in Russellville, Arkansas; and the folks at the Newton County Courthouse in Jasper, Arkansas.

I thank my children who have survived (not without some complaining) the telling and retelling of many of these stories in our family circle. It came to the point that when I would begin a tale, the gals (Cyndi, Celia, and Cheri) would chorus, "Way back in the hills. . . ."

Beyond and above all, I thank my dear and beloved Marti, a gifted writer in her own right, who has taught me more about storytelling than all the editors and professors under whom I have labored. We are different in a hundred and one ways, but we are alike in our love and commitment to one another.

Finally, I present these hopes: that my kith and kin will better understand my experience with God; that my children and their children will be brought in closer touch with their roots; that the memories of Big Creek Valley and grandpas and grandmas and uncles and aunts of years past will better be remembered and cherished as a result of what has been penned in these pages.

Other Living Books Best-sellers